The
English
Patient

The

Based on the novel by Michael Ondaatje

English Patient

A screenplay by Anthony Minghella

METHUEN FILM

A METHUEN SCREENPLAY

First published in Great Britain in 1997
by Methuen Drama
an imprint of Reed International Books Ltd
Michelin House, 81 Fulham Road, London SW3 6RB
and Auckland, Melbourne, Singapore and Toronto

Reprinted 1997

A CIP catalogue record for this book
is available from the British Library
ISBN 0 413 71500 0

Typeset in Palatino and Goudy Old Style
by Wilmaset Ltd, Birkenhead, Wirral

for Carolyn

Foreword

When I was a child films felt like wondrous news and emotion from another planet and I had to be dragged from the Regal Cinema in Colombo at the end of *The Four Feathers*. When I became a writer I continued to love films because they *were* completely different from books. Movies not only used different materials, they had different cooking times for their great soups, and had to be consumed in public alongside eight hundred other people as opposed to by one solitary diner. A film was closer to the simulated excitement of a soccer stadium while books were a meditative and private act – you sat down to read one or write one and the first thing you did was ignore the rest of the world. Whereas film had various sous-chefs and a studio and a market to deal with. A book could be secret as a canoe trip, the making of a film more like the voyage of *Lord Jim*'s Patna – uncertain of ever reaching its destination with a thousand pilgrims on board and led by a morally dubious crew. But somehow, magically, it now and then got to a safe harbour.

I knew this before getting involved with Saul Zaentz and Anthony Minghella and I knew I was lucky to work with them. Saul more than anyone knew the woes and joys of adapting novels and plays into film. He had steered *One Flew Over the Cuckoo's Nest*, *Amadeus*, and *The Unbearable Lightness of Being*, among others, into the cinema. And while Anthony is a wonderful director he is, first and always, a writer. Like Saul he treasures books. Leaving an editing room we would often decompress by scurrying into a bookstore in Berkeley.

Still, right from the start, all three of us never wanted the film of *The English Patient* to be a dutiful version of the book. None of us wanted just a faithful echo. I knew my story's shape and various swerves and plots would not go unscathed. There would be translations of form and emphasis. Saul slipped me a copy of the short story that *Rear Window* was based on and I was horrified to discover that Grace Kelly's character did not exist in it. If the film had followed the story it would have been about James Stewart and his manservant. All this was, I knew, a warning on Saul's part before I saw the first draft.

At our first script meeting, we had hardly begun when Saul pointed to the first paragraph. 'What's this?' Buried in the description of the pilot clambering out of a burning plane was the word 'plangent'. 'It's . . .' Anthony began. 'I know what it means, but if you give this to a studio to read they'll fling it away.' 'Plangent' was the first word removed from the various drafts over the next three years. What was more difficult for Anthony was what had to be cut out later . . . those scenes that sparkled and glistened but which did not fit the dramatic time lines of a film.

If one writes a great chapter in a novel, it will seldom be taken out of a book for reasons of time or rhythm. A novel allows you longer arms, a deeper breath. Anthony's scenes of Kip in England, which were wonderful and haunting, did not survive. Time spent on that flashback would have diverted the audience from the main plot for too long, and seeing Kip's bomb defusing work would have held no tension because we would know he had survived it. In the novel we are more within the meditations of Kip as he works on several bombs – but these were some of the passages and nuances that film could not carry. For the film Kip's bomb work had to be live, in the present, in Italy. There were other losses in the translation to film but in each case they were understandable choices. They also made the film better.

For me, the long roots of Hana's and Caravaggio's psyches, Kip's training in England, his reaction to the atomic bomb, and his eventual fate, will always remain in the original country of the novel. What we have now are two stories, one with the intimate pace and detail of a three-hundred-page novel, and one that is the length of a vivid and subtle film. Each has its own organic structure. There are obvious differences and values but somehow each version deepens the other.

Both Saul and Anthony fought with everything they had for the kind of film they believed in, for the cast they wanted – even when it might have meant abandonment by a studio. What they took from the book was its spirit and they always protected that. One day when they were shooting a Cairo taxi scene, someone came up to Anthony and said, 'I'm so glad you kept the taxi scene from the book.' He received a slow burn from Anthony as there had never been a taxi scene in the book. This happened often. And what is most interesting to me about the film now is how scenes and emotions and values from the book emerged in new ways, were re-invented, were invented with totally new moments, and fit within a dramatic arc that was different from the arc of the book. Quite honestly now the territories and maps are blurred as to what is new, what was mine, what was Anthony's, what was Saul or Ralph Fiennes or Juliette Binoche, what was Walter Murch. You have a communal story made by many hands.

Anthony and Saul were always in the centre. From the first time we met in the fall of 1992 till now, while they are in the last stages of the film, they have carried the project. They have spent most waking hours on this story with more love and care than I've seen given to any project I've been involved with. For Anthony especially, the project was obsessive: working on sets in Rome, flying to L.A. during a crisis, rewriting, breaking his ankle during the filming and not even taking the afternoon off, rewriting, and directing the actors with great intimacy and honesty.

What held us was that something new and different was emerging. The characters grew in Anthony's script, speaking the way I imagined they would speak. And when the actors arrived they too brought their individual sense and senses to the characters and gave them those glances and gestures that came from their own imaginations.

It is as if people I knew when I was writing a book at

midnight, full of dreams, now appear in a new country in daylight and the wonder is not so much of how they made that magical journey but that I recognize them so well and that I am once again enthralled by them. That was the gift I never expected.

Michael Ondaatje
Toronto, July 1996

Preface

The English Patient was the first book of Michael Ondaatje's I had read, and I thought it was remarkable. Two weeks after finishing the novel, Anthony Minghella telephoned from London and asked, 'How could we do this as a movie?' Being a cagy, wily, veteran producer, I pirouetted around him with, 'How could *you* do this as a movie?' I don't think he had a single idea.

The first draft that Anthony sent me a year later had many practical problems: it had too many countries, too many characters, and was 185 pages long. But it demonstrated that there was a way to transform an incredibly complex novel into film. Over the course of the next year working between London and my home in Northern California, and ploughing between several drafts, the screenplay continued to shed pages, characters, and scenes that we loved. And it kept improving. All good screenwriters begin with what they think is necessary and end up with what are necessities. The process continues into the editing room, where an actor's performance can be so sublime and communicative that whole scenes become redundant. Michael Ondaatje came to California after each draft to collaborate with us. And when, in September 1995, after the many, many difficulties we encountered getting *The English Patient* financed, we were finally making the movie, he came to our locations in Italy and the Sahara. He had ideas that Anthony acknowledged he would never have thought of and they were received with open arms. Michael has been a friend throughout the writing, filming, and editing.

A part of this script was created during production. All through filming Anthony would come up with marvellously filmic ideas, not the kind which involve hiring fifty movie extras, but adjustments to tailor his material to what we found in our actors or in our locations, to make something more personal or particular.

Anthony is the best director with actors I've ever worked with. He understands their parts, respects them, and speaks their language. Good actors, and we had them, come to the set bringing wonderful things, and a really good director recognizes these gifts and knows how to use them without fear.

Saul Zaentz
Berkeley, Summer 1996

Introduction

I first read *The English Patient* in a single gulp, sitting in a room on 77th and Columbus the morning after I'd finished a sweltering summer of filming in New York. When I put the book down, it was dark, and I had no idea where I was.

Michael Ondaatje's novel has the deceptive appearance of being completely cinematic. Brilliant images are scattered across its pages in a mosaic of fractured narratives, as if somebody had already seen a film and was in a hurry trying to remember all the best bits. In the course of a single page, the reader can be asked to consider events in Cairo, or Tuscany, or England's west country during different periods, with different narrators; to meditate on the nature of winds, the mischief of an elbow, the intricacies of a bomb mechanism, the significance of a cave painting. The wise screen adapter approaches such pages with extreme caution. The fool rushes in. The next morning I telephoned Saul Zaentz in Berkeley, the only producer I could think of crazy enough to countenance such a project, and suggested he read the book. He's made a brilliant career out of folly, and is one of the few movie-makers who loves to read. I have never seen Saul without a book within his reach. He called me back a week after to tell me not only did he love *The English Patient*, but that Michael was coming in from Toronto to give a reading from it that weekend at a bookstore near Saul's home. I encouraged him to see this as an omen.

When I began work on the screenplay, a number of things were immediately evident – I was completely ignorant about Egypt, had never been to a desert, couldn't use a compass, couldn't read a map, remembered nothing from my schoolboy history lessons about the Second World

War, and embarrassingly little about Italy, my parents' country. I promptly borrowed a cottage in Durweston, Dorset, and loaded up my car with books. I began adult life as an academic and nothing gives me more pleasure than the opportunity to tell myself that reading is a serious activity. I waded through eccentric books on military history, letters and diaries of soldiers in North Africa and Southern Italy, pamphlets from the Royal Geographical Society written before the war. I found out about the devastation visited on my father's village near Monte Cassino, discovered we had a namesake who was a partisan leader in Tuscany, learned about the incredible international crucible that was Cairo in the 1930s.

The one book I didn't take with me was *The English Patient*. I had been so mesmerized by the writing, so steeped in its richness, that I decided the only possible course available was to try and write my way back to the concerns of the novel, telling myself its story. I emerged from my purdah with a first draft of over two hundred pages (twice the length of a conventional screenplay) which included, even after my own rough edit and much to the bewilderment of my collaborators, episodes involving goat mutilation, scores of new characters, and a scene about the destruction of a wisteria tree in Dorset which I swore privately would be the most memorable in the film. Needless to say, none of these inventions survived to the first day of principal photography. Over successive drafts – each of which were subject to the ruthless, exasperating, egoless, pedantic, and rigorous scrutiny of Michael and Saul – some kind of blueprint for a film began to emerge. We met in California, Toronto, London, and, best of all, in Saul's home in Tuscany where I am ashamed to admit there were memorable discussions held in the cool, aquamarine pool, our chins bobbing on the surface of the water, punctuated by bouts of what we called water polo but which was essentially a form of licensed violence to work off all our various pent-up hostilities, and at which Michael proved to be the master.

Numerous people made this screenplay better, notably

Maura Dooley (who had, several years previously, introduced me to Michael's work), Sydney Pollack, Evgenia Citkowitz, Julian Sands, Michael Peretzian, Judy Daish, Alan Rickman, Sarah Ewing, Annette Carducci, Walter Murch, and Ralph Fiennes. I'd also like to thank Duncan Kenworthy for providing me a safe haven to write, the Royal Geographical Society in London for allowing me access to photographs and papers, Andrew Phillips at the British Library for unearthing a particular treasure, and Saul Zaentz for being the kind of producer that writers and directors kneel down and thank God for. Then, of course, there is an entire cast and crew, listed elsewhere here, who have lent their skills and passion to this material as it moved from script to screen. My heartfelt gratitude to them all.

One significant aspect of this published text is the extent to which it differs from the script I began shooting with. The evolution of the material has continued in post-production as scenes have been compressed or eliminated and, in particular, the structure of the film – with its transitions between events in Egypt and in Italy – has been radically revised. Walter Murch, the film's editor, must take special credit for this, and our collaboration gives real meaning to the observation that the writing process continues in the editing room.

I hope the army of admirers of Michael Ondaatje's novel forgive my sins of omission and commission, my misjudgments and betrayals; they were all made in the spirit of translating his beautiful novel to the screen. I was determined and encouraged to have my say about the people and events described in the book, and was obliged to make transparent what was delicately oblique in the prose. It seemed to me that the process of adaptation required me to join the dots and make a figurative work from a pointillist and abstract one. Any number of versions were possible and I'm certain that the stories I chose to elaborate say as much about my own interests and reading as they do about the book. And I can't apologize for this. It's a testimony to Michael's enormous modesty that he presided over the process with neither indifference nor contempt, and continues to lend his wit and intelligence to us as the film nears the moment of what we call completion but which is only abandonment.

Anthony Minghella
July 1996

THE
ENGLISH
PATIENT

Ext. The Sahara Desert. Late 1942

Silence. The desert seen from the air. An ocean of dunes for mile after mile. The late sun turns the sand every colour from crimson to black and makes the dunes look like bodies pressed against each other.

An old aeroplane is flying over the Sahara. Its shadow swims over the contours of sand.

A woman's voice begins to sing — Szerelem, szerelem, she cries, in a haunting lament for her loved one.

Inside the aeroplane are two figures. One, a woman, seems to be asleep. Her pale head rests against the side of the cockpit. Behind her the Pilot, a man, wears goggles and a leather helmet. He is singing, too, but we can't hear him or the plane or anything save the singer's plaintive voice.

The plane shudders over a ridge. Beneath it a sudden cluster of men and machines, camouflage nets draped over the sprawl of gasoline tanks and armoured vehicles. An officer, German, focuses his field glasses. The glasses pick out the markings on the plane. They are in English. An anti-aircraft gun swivels furiously.

Shocking bursts of gunfire. Explosions rock the plane, which lurches violently. The fuel tank is punctured. It

3

sprays out gasoline, then erupts in flame engulfing both figures in a fireball.

Int. Train. Italy 1944. Before dawn

An allied hospital train ploughs through the night carrying military wounded back to Naples.

A young French-Canadian nurse, HANA, walks through a long carriage past rows of the injured. She stops at the bunk of a wounded soldier. HANA bends to the BOY. He's had shrapnel in his legs and cheek. She speaks softly to him.

> HANA

How are you?

> BOY

Okay.

> HANA

Your leg will be fine. A lot of shrapnel came out
– I saved you the pieces.

> BOY

You're the prettiest girl I've ever seen.

> HANA
> *(she hears this every day)*

I don't think so.

> BOY

Would you kiss me?

> HANA

No, I'll get you some tea.

BOY
(innocent)
It would mean such a lot to me.

HANA
(tender, believing him)
Would it?

She kisses him, very softly, on the lips.

BOY
Thank you.

He closes his eyes. HANA smiles, continues along the
compartment. Teasing voices call out after her.

#1 INJURED MAN
Nurse – I can't sleep.

#2 INJURED MAN
Would you kiss me?

#3 INJURED MAN
You're so pretty!

HANA
(good-naturedly waving away their joke)
Very funny. Go to sleep now.

She opens the door of the next carriage and walks straight
into the carnage left by an emergency operation. MARY,
another nurse, is removing a blood-soaked bundle from the
operating table. MARY grimaces.

MARY
Don't ask.

Ext. The desert. Day

The Pilot has been rescued by Bedouin tribesmen. Behind them the wreckage of the plane, still smoking, the Arabs picking over it. A silver thimble glints in the sun, is retrieved. Another man comes across a large leather-bound book and takes it over to where the Pilot is being tended to. The book is full of letters and cards and paintings. They're scattering everywhere. The Pilot is terribly burned, barely alive, his face charred. One of the Bedouins covers his face with a makeshift mask made from plaited palm leaves.

Ext. The desert. Dusk

The Pilot is being carried across the desert. The mask covers his face. His view of the world is through the slats of palm. He glimpses camels, fierce low sun, the men who carry him.

Ext. Emergency Field Hospital, 1944. Late day

The Emergency Field Hospital is a cluster of tents practically ahead of the Front Line. Sporadic gunfire, increasingly near, sounds throughout. It's 1944 and the war in Italy is still intense.

Int. Main triage tent, Emergency Field Hospital. Night

HANA *and her best friend,* JAN, *walk through the main triage tent. It's packed with the ruined bodies of the injured, swaddled in bloody bandages.*

Int. Triage tent, Emergency Field Hospital. Evening

HANA *is giving blood. She lies in a cot, next to* JAN. *The shelling sounds closer.*

Behind a curtain, OLIVER, *a doctor, is working on the most recent patient, a young* CANADIAN SOLDIER *who is critically ill — the tubes hanging above him, of plasma and of blood, his stomach a bloody mess. The curtain drawn around him is pulled back to reveal the two nurses in background. The* SOLDIER *can just see them. He's going to die any minute.*

CANADIAN SOLDIER
(*whispering to* OLIVER)
Is there anybody from Picton?

OLIVER
Picton? I don't know.

CANADIAN SOLDIER
I'd like to see somebody from home before I go.

HANA *can only really hear* OLIVER'*s end of this conversation, but the mention of Picton chills her, and she knows, now, not later, that her lover is dead.*

HANA
(*to* OLIVER)
Why Picton?

OLIVER
He's from there – edge of Lake Ontario, right, Soldier?

The boy nods.

JAN
(*innocent*)
Hey, that's where your sweetie's from?
Somewhere near there, isn't it?

HANA
(to OLIVER)
Ask him what company he's with.

OLIVER *leans over, then turns to* HANA.

OLIVER
Third Canadian Fusiliers.

HANA
Does he know a Captain McGann?

The boy hears this, whispers to OLIVER.

CANADIAN SOLDIER
He bought it. Yesterday. Shot to bits.

The shells are getting closer.

HANA
What did he say?

OLIVER
(can't look at her)
Doesn't know him.

A shell suddenly lands on top of the site, perhaps fifty yards from the tent. The lights go out. Then another lands.

Everybody is on the floor, struggling to get on a helmet. HANA lies down, the blood still leaving her, her helmet on. OLIVER is next to her in the mud. Her heart is breaking.

HANA
He's gone, he's gone, he's gone.

OLIVER

No. He's – no.

HANA

Oh God. Oh God.

The shells pound them, incredibly loud, drowning out her grief, but each explosion illuminates it for a moment.

Ext. An oasis. Night

The sound of glass, of tiny chimes. A music of glass.

An Arab head floats in darkness, shimmering from the light of a fire. The image develops to reveal a man carrying a large wooden yoke from which hang dozens of small glass bottles, on different lengths of string and wire. He could be an angel.

The man approaches the litter which carries the Pilot. He's still in the protective palm mask, wrapped in blankets. The Merchant Doctor stands over the burned body and sinks sticks either side of him deep into the sand, then moves away, free of the yoke, which balances in the support of the two crutches. Then he slowly sets about peeling away the layers of oiled cloth which protect the Pilot's flesh.

The Merchant Doctor crouches in front of the curtain of bottles, then leans back to pluck, hardly looking, certain bottles which he uncorks and mixes. He uses this green-black paste to anoint the burned skin. All the while he is humming and chanting. The bottles continue to jingle.

Ext. Beach front, Italy. Late 1944. Day

Wounded soldiers walk with nurses along the beach.

Ext. Beach cabins, Italy. Late 1944. Day

This convalescence hospital has been fashioned from a long row of bathing cabins on the coast, complete with Campari umbrellas and metal tables, at which are seated the bandaged and the dying and the comatose, staring out to sea or in slow, muted conversation. A BRITISH OFFICER makes notes. He is talking to a wounded PATIENT, whom we recognize as the burned Pilot.

OFFICER (o/s)
Name? Rank? Serial number?

THE PATIENT (o/s)
No. Sorry. I think I was a pilot. I was found near the wreckage of a plane at the beginning of the War.

HANA walks up to THE PATIENT's cabin. He is propped up with a view of the sea, which is interrupted by the BRITISH OFFICER. HANA has a blanket and a chart for THE PATIENT's bed. She busies herself.

OFFICER
Can you remember where you were born?

THE PATIENT
Am I being interrogated? You should be trying to trick me. Or make me speak German, which I can, by the way.

OFFICER
Why? Are you German?

THE PATIENT
No.

OFFICER

How do you know you're not German if you
don't remember anything?

THE PATIENT

Might I have a sip of water?

HANA *pours him a glass of water. He notices her.*

THE PATIENT

Thank you.
(*he sips*)
I remember lots of things. I remember a garden,
plunging down to the sea – nothing between you
and France.

OFFICER

This was your garden?

THE PATIENT

Or my wife's.

OFFICER

Then you were married?

THE PATIENT

I think so. Although I believe that to be true of
a number of Germans. Look –
(*makes a small gap with his fingers*)
I have this much lung . . . the rest of my organs
are packing up – what could it possibly matter if
I were *Tutankhamen*? I'm a bit of toast, my friend
– butter me and slip a poached egg on top.

Ext. Italian hill road. Day

A convoy of twenty trucks – Red Cross vehicles and some

supply vehicles – snakes along a bumpy hill road. The war
in Italy is largely over and the Allies are moving up the
country, the wounded and supply lines slowly following.

Ext. Italian hill road. Day

A jeep pulls out of the line and approaches the Red Cross
truck containing HANA and THE PATIENT. The horn
blows and HANA looks out to see it contains her friend
JAN. Two young soldiers sit up front, one driving, both
grinning. JAN signals for HANA's attention.

> JAN
>
> Hana! Hana! Hana! There's meant to be lace in
> the next village – the boys are going to take me.
> > (mischievously)
> You don't have any money, do you? Just in case
> there's silk.

> HANA
>
> No!

> JAN
>
> Hana, I know you do. Come on. Oh, come on.
> > (to the soldiers)
> She's a softy, she loves me.

HANA leans under the tarpaulin, holding some dollars.
The two hands – hers and JAN's – reach for each other as
the vehicles bump along side by side. They laugh at the
effort. JAN's gold bracelet catches the sun and glints.

> JAN
> > (getting the money)
> I love you.

The jeep accelerates away. HANA sighs to THE PATIENT.

Suddenly an explosion shatters the calm as the jeep runs over a mine. The jeep is thrown into the air. The convoy halts and there's chaos as soldiers run back pulling people out of the vehicles. HANA runs the other way, toward the accident, until she is prevented from reaching JAN's mangled body by the consoling arms of OLIVER.

Ext. Italian hill road. Later

– and there's still chaos as two sappers (Bomb Disposal Squad) work on the road ahead. One of them, a Sikh, wears a turban.

Ext. Italian hill road. Day

KIP, the Sikh lieutenant, and HARDY, his sergeant, explore the road ahead of the becalmed convoy, using saucer-like metal detectors and headsets. KIP is young, lithe, contained, utterly focused as they inch along the debris-strewn road. He stiffens as he registers metal. With a bayonet he carefully scrapes at the mud-caked surface. Something gleams. Suddenly, a pair of feet walk across his vision as HANA hurries past, walking carelessly up the road. It's so surreal that neither man registers at first, and then KIP is shouting.

> KIP
> Hey! Hey! Stop! Hey!

Now HARDY is shouting for her to stop. HANA looks around.

> HARDY
> Don't move. Stand ABSOLUTELY STILL!

HANA stops. HARDY gingerly follows her footsteps.

HARDY
(*as he approaches*)

Good, that's good, just stay still for me and then
we'll be fine.

He arrives at HANA. *Then grabs her. He'd like to slap her
face.*

HARDY

What are you doing? What the bloody hell do
you think you're doing?

*By way of answer she looks at the ground ahead of her
feet.* JAN's *bracelet lies in the mud.* HARDY *bends down
and collects the mangled bracelet, presses it into* HANA's
hands.

Ext. Village. Dusk

*The convoy is threading through a ruined village, passing
the souvenirs of war: an overturned vehicle now used as a
game by some children; dejected refugees tramping along
the side of the road.*

Int. Red Cross truck. Continuous

HANA sees all this as she sits blankly inside the truck, THE
PATIENT *swaying alongside her. She puts out her hand to
steady him. Tears streak her face.*

Ext. Convoy site, Italy. Dusk

*The convoy is making a pit stop. The trucks are
silhouetted in a line.* HANA *helps lift* THE PATIENT's
stretcher onto the ground. She bends to him. HANA *gets
up to prepare a morphine injection from a small kit.* MARY

14

arrives. Touches HANA *gently, conscious of her grief for* JAN's *death.*

MARY
Are you okay? Oh God, Hana, you and Jan were
inseparable.

HANA
(*sighs angrily*)
We keep moving him – in and out of the truck.
Why? He's dying. What's the point?

MARY
(*thrown*)
Do you mean leave him? We can't. We can
hardly leave him.

HANA *has settled down beside* THE PATIENT's *stretcher.
She draws herself up against the night. On the hill above,
she can see the outline of a small monastery in the
moonlight. She's suffering, her face a frozen mask.*

HANA
I must be a curse – anybody who loves me,
anybody who gets close to me – or I must be
cursed. Which is it?

THE PATIENT *laces her fingers into his crabbed hand.*

Ext. The monastery. Day

HANA *is investigating the Monastery of S. Anna,
wandering through its overgrown gardens, past a pond.
What sanctuary it seems to offer.*

Int. The monastery library. Day

HANA *explores via a gaping hole in a library where the walls have collapsed from shelling. The garden intrudes, ivy curls around the shelves. Bloated books lie abandoned, and there's a piano tilted up on one side. HANA presses the keys through the filthy tarpaulin which covers it. Everywhere there are signs of a brief German occupation.*

Int. The monastery cloisters. Day

Past the library is a cloisters, drenched with silver light.

Int. The monastery stairs. Day

HANA *goes upstairs, negotiating a huge void in the stone treads two thirds of the way up.*

Int. The Patient's room. Day

She comes across a small chapel with the remains of murals and an altar pressed into service by the Germans as a table. HANA *finds an old bed and a mattress.*

Ext. Convoy site, Italy. Day

The convoy is in the final stages of loading up. OLIVER *passes the vehicles, deep in dispute with a determined* HANA, *who is carrying some sacks of rice.*

HANA
When he dies I'll catch up.

OLIVER
I can't allow it. It's not safe here. The whole country's crawling with Bandits and Germans and God knows what.

HANA

The war's over – you told me yourself. How can
it be desertion?

OLIVER

It's not over everywhere. I didn't mean literally.
This is normal – it's shock. For all of us. Hana –

OLIVER *hovers as* HANA *adds the rice to a small cache of
provisions then lays another blanket over* THE PATIENT.

HANA

I need morphine. A lot. And a pistol.

OLIVER

If anything happened to you I'd never forgive
myself.

HANA *nods. A tiny smile.* OLIVER *shrugs helplessly.*

OLIVER

We're heading for Leghorn. *Livorno*, the Italians
call it. We'll expect you.

Int. The Patient's room. Day

Two soldiers are helping MARY *and* HANA *carry* THE
PATIENT *into what was the chapel. They lower* THE
PATIENT *onto the rusted bed.* HANA *turns to the soldiers.*

HANA

Thank you.

She shuts the door on them, leaving MARY *staring aghast
at the room, its faded frescoes, its mould, its starkness.*

HANA

Good.

She goes to MARY *and hugs her.*

Int. The monastery, Hana's room. Day

A smaller upstairs room, completely bare. As HANA *tugs off her uniform, she looks out of the window to see the departing convoy. A cotton dress goes on over her head and she emerges looking suddenly younger and rather fragile. Through the damaged floor of her room she has a view of* THE PATIENT *below her. She looks at him. Now she has scissors and starts to cut off her hair, not aggressively, but in a gesture of a new beginning.*

Int. The monastery stairs. Morning

HANA *is dropping armfuls of books into the cavities of the damaged stairs while, with others, she is improvising new steps. The heavy volumes are perfect for treading on.*

Int. The Patient's room. Day

HANA *enters.*

THE PATIENT

What was all the banging? Were you fighting rats or the entire German army?

HANA

I was repairing the stairs. I found a library and the books were very useful.

HANA *shrugs. She's attending to him, pulling back the sheets, plumping up the pillows. He's short of breath.*

19

THE PATIENT

Before you find too many uses for these books
would you read some to me?

HANA

I think they're all in Italian, but I'll look, yes.
What about your own book?

THE PATIENT
(*reluctant*)
My book? The *Herodotus*? Yes, we can read him.

HANA *picks up the book from the altar and hands it to
him. Then she starts rummaging in her pockets.*

HANA

Oh – I've found plums. We have plums in the
orchard. We have an orchard!

THE PATIENT

Herodotus is the father of history, do you know
that?

HANA

I don't know anything.

THE PATIENT

Thank you.

*She has peeled a plum and now slips it into his mouth. His
mouth works with the pleasure of the taste, a little juice
escaping from his lips.* HANA *mops it up.*

THE PATIENT

It's a very *plum* plum.

Ext. The monastery gardens. Day

HANA sits in the water trough shivering as the cold water splashes her.

Int. The Patient's room. Day

Close on the Herodotus. THE PATIENT opens its cover, held together by leather ties. Loose papers, photographs, hand-drawn maps, and sketches are all collected between the charred pages. He claws at some papers, inspects a letter. Then he loses control of the papers and the whole parcel spills to the floor with a crack.

Ext. Base Camp at Pottery Hill. Dusk

COUNT LASZLO DE ALMÁSY, Hungarian explorer, squats with an ancient Arab who draws in the sand, talking in some arcane dialect, scratching out a map. The old man stops speaking and scours the sky a beat or two before we or ALMÁSY hear the faint noise of a plane. It's a bright yellow Steerman coming in to land. ALMÁSY doesn't look up. The Arab continues to talk. The plane sweeps past the cluster of tents and camels and trucks which constitutes the Base Camp for a team of international explorers, led by ALMÁSY and his colleague, PETER MADOX.

Ext. Base Camp at Pottery Hill. Day

The expedition team drives over to meet the arrivals. ALMÁSY stays in the car as the others pile out and approach the plane as it taxis alongside an old, battered, silver Tiger Moth.

A young couple emerge from the Steerman. They are GEOFFREY and KATHARINE CLIFTON.

And it's immediately clear that KATHARINE *is the woman in the plane crash at the beginning of the film.*

MADOX *makes all the introductions, introducing the rest of the team – an Italian,* D'AGOSTINO; *a German* BERMANN; *and an Egyptian,* FOUAD. *Hands are shaken, hellos all around, as the couple disembark in their leather flying gear.*

Ext. Base Camp at Pottery Hill. Late day

The party is in the shade of the tents. GEOFFREY CLIFTON *produces a bottle of champagne and sets off the cork with a flourish.* ALMÁSY *joins the group.* MADOX *nods over to the* CLIFTON *plane.*

CLIFTON
To the International Sand Club.

MADOX
Marvellous plane. Did you look?

ALMÁSY
Yes.

CLIFTON
(*beaming at* ALMÁSY)
Isn't it? Wedding present from Katharine's
parents. We're calling it Rupert Bear. Hello.
Geoffrey Clifton.

MADOX
(*of his plane*)
We can finally consign my old bird to the scrap
heap.

ALMÁSY *smiles and walks on toward the others.*

23

D'AGOSTINO
Mrs Clifton – Count Almásy.

KATHARINE
(*smiling, offering her hand*)
Hello. Geoffrey gave me your monograph when
I was reading up on the desert. Very impressive.

ALMÁSY
(*stiff*)
Thank you.

KATHARINE
I wanted to meet a man who could write such a
long paper with so few adjectives.

ALMÁSY
A thing is still a thing no matter what you place
in front of it. Big car, slow car, chauffeur-driven
car – still a car.

CLIFTON
(*joining them and joining in*)
A broken car?

ALMÁSY
Still a car.

CLIFTON
(*hands them champagne*)
Not much use, though.

KATHARINE
Love? Romantic love, platonic love, filial love – ?
Quite different things, surely?

CLIFTON
(*hugging* KATHARINE)
Uxoriousness – that's my favourite kind of love.
Excessive love of one's wife.

ALMÁSY
(*a dry smile*)
Now there you have me.

Ext. Base Camp. Morning

ALMÁSY *and* MADOX *head for* MADOX's *Tiger Moth.*
They turn the machine around like a toy, pointing it in the
right direction for take-off. During this ALMÁSY *complains*
and MADOX *mediates – there's a suspicion that this is a*
familiar dynamic.

ALMÁSY
They're tourists.

MADOX
Absolute rot. They come highly recommended
from the Royal Geographic. She's charming and
has read everything, he's meant to be a ruddy
good pilot.

ALMÁSY
We don't need another pilot.

MADOX
He can make aerial maps of the entire area.

ALMÁSY
You can't explore from the air, Madox. If you
could explore from the air, life would be very
simple.
(*he primes the propeller*)

Contact.

MADOX *slips on his goggles and turns on the engine.*

                    MADOX
Contact.

ALMÁSY *spins the propeller. It flashes into life.*

Ext. Gilf Kebir Plateau. Morning

Both planes are scouting the Gilf Kebir region. GEOFFREY *flies up alongside* MADOX *and wiggles his wings.* MADOX *waves. They're flying over a distinctive group of granite massifs, crater-shaped hills. The broken towers of the Gilf Kebir.* ALMÁSY *is distracted by them. He turns to* MADOX *and points down, indicating they should explore them.*

MADOX *nods and brings the plane lower and they fly into the mouth of one of the huge craters. The* CLIFTONS' *plane follows them into the black ravines, pitted with signs of scrub.*

ALMÁSY *gestures to the* CLIFTONS *to photograph the Massifs. A thumbs up from* GEOFFREY, *who pulls out his camera and begins shooting.*

Int. The Patient's room. Morning

HANA *changes* THE PATIENT'S *bed. The light streams in from the open window. She looks up at the green hills rolling away from the monastery, the village in the distance.*

HANA
I should try and move the bed. I want you to be able to see the view. It's good, it's a view from a monastery.

THE PATIENT
I can already see.

HANA
(bending down to his level)
How? How can you see anything?

THE PATIENT
No, not the window – I can't bear the light anyway – no, I can see all the way to the desert. Before the war. Making maps.

HANA
I'm turning you.

THE PATIENT
Is there sand in my eyes? Are you cleaning sand from my ears?

HANA
No sand, that's your morphine speaking.

THE PATIENT
I can see my wife in that view.

HANA
Are you remembering more?

THE PATIENT
Could I have a cigarette?

27

> HANA

Are you crazy?

> THE PATIENT

Why are you so determined to keep me alive?

> HANA

Because I'm a nurse.

Ext. The monastery cloisters. Night

It's dark. HANA is caught by the stray shafts of moonlight. She is scratching on the flagstones. Her skirt is bunched up around her thighs. She throws something in the air. It lands with a crack. Suddenly she is flying across the space, a hop, a skip, a jump. Then turns at the other end, dips for the stone, then back again, in this blindman's version of hopscotch.

Int. The Patient's room. Night

Alone in his room THE PATIENT listens to the erratic rhythm of HANA's hopscotch. It takes him back to the desert and the sound of Bedouin drums on a night shortly after the arrival of the CLIFTONS.

Ext. Base Camp. Night

The group sits around the campfire at night, supper over, champagne drunk. They're using the empty bottle to play a game – Spin the Bottle. When the bottle points at you, you're required to perform a party piece. CLIFTON sings a version of 'Yes, We Have No Bananas', then is required to translate it into a variety of languages – the others joining in raucously. D'AGOSTINO offers a Puccini aria; FOUAD dances, his shawl whirling, the Bedouin onlookers providing a percussive, improvised accompaniment.

Int. The Patient's room. Night

Later, and HANA *is reading to* THE PATIENT *from a story in his Herodotus. As she reads, he listens, eyes closed, still in the desert.*

> HANA
> . . . the King insisted he would find some way to prove beyond dispute that his wife was fairest of all women. 'I will hide you in the room where we sleep,' says Candaules –
> > *(correcting herself)*
> – said Candaules.

She stumbles over the word. THE PATIENT *corrects her.*

> THE PATIENT
> Candaules.

> HANA
> Candaules.

Ext. Base Camp at Pottery Hill. Night

KATHARINE *has her turn at the fire. She is telling the same story.* THE PATIENT *remembers her.*

> KATHARINE
> Candaules tells Gyges that the queen has the same practice every night. She takes off her clothes and puts them on the chair by the door to her room . . .

> HANA (o/s)
> *(continuing to read)*
> . . . and from where you stand you will be able to gaze on her at your leisure . . .

KATHARINE
(*her story continuing*)
And that evening it's exactly as the King has
told him. She goes to the chair and removes her
clothes one by one until she's standing naked in
full view of Gyges, and indeed she was more
lovely than he could have imagined. But then
the Queen looked up and saw Gyges concealed
in the shadows, and although she said nothing,
she shuddered. And the next day she sent for
Gyges and challenged him. And hearing his
story, this is what she said –

CLIFTON
(*clowning*)
Off with his head!

KATHARINE
– she said, 'Either you must submit to death for
gazing on that which you should not, or else kill
my husband who shamed me and become King
in his place.'

CLIFTON *makes a face of outrage. For* KATHARINE *the
story has suddenly collapsed. She feels* ALMÁSY's *eyes on
her.*

KATHARINE
So Gyges kills the King and marries the Queen
and becomes ruler of Lydia for twenty-eight
years.
(*an uncomfortable moment*)
Shall I spin the bottle?

The others laugh. MADOX *beams at* CLIFTON.

MADOX
So Geoffrey – let that be a lesson to you.

Int. The Patient's room. Night

HANA *looks up from the* Herodotus, *sees* THE PATIENT'S *eyes closed. She gently touches his face and whispers.*

HANA
Are you asleep?

THE PATIENT
(*he isn't*)
Yes. No. Dropping off.

And HANA *closes the book, gets up, kisses him good night, and blows out the lamp.*

Ext. The monastery, Hana's garden. Late day

HANA *has been reviving a vegetable patch. She comes out to garden. Crows are feasting. She's furious, shouts, runs at them. Nature, wildness, insisting on invading her peace.*

Ext. The monastery, graveyard. Morning

HANA *appears from the cemetery, dragging a metal crucifix. It's bigger than she is, and she drags it along toward her garden. A man watches her from a bicycle. He's approaching fifty, grizzled and attractive, and could be Italian. He wears a pair of grubby mittens. The man,* CARAVAGGIO, *chooses this moment to introduce himself. He drops the bicycle on the ground with a clatter.*

CARAVAGGIO
(*very cheerful*)
Buon giorno!

HANA *turns, startled and suspicious.*

CARAVAGGIO

Hana?

HANA

What do you want?

CARAVAGGIO

I met your friend Mary. She said I should stop
and see if you were all right. Apparently, we're
neighbours – my house is two blocks from yours
in Montreal. Cabot, north of Laurier. *Bonjour.*

HANA
(unravelling this information)

Bonjour.

*He goes to her and hands her an egg, producing it from a
pocket. He beams, as does HANA.*

CARAVAGGIO

I'd like to take credit for it, but it's from Mary.
My name's David Caravaggio, but nobody ever
called me David. Caravaggio – they find too
absurd to miss out on.

*During this he attempts to conjure a second egg from
HANA's ear. The egg drops to the ground. Cursing, he
gets on his knees and starts to scoop it up, preserving it.
There appears to be something wrong with his hands. He
grimaces at HANA.*

CARAVAGGIO

My stupid hands!

33

Int. The monastery kitchen. Day

HANA *has taken his eggs and put them into a bowl. She beats them with a knife, picking out the bits of shell.* CARAVAGGIO *watches, takes in how little food there is otherwise. The table seems useful more as a sewing area than for cooking – it's strewn with altar cloths being sewn into drapes. On a tray on the table are two vials of morphine from* THE PATIENT'S *room. As* HANA *turns to the stove,* CARAVAGGIO'S *moved and covered them with his gloved hands; a second later and he's juggled them into his pocket.*

CARAVAGGIO
(*of the eggs*)
They're fresh. I haven't had an egg in . . . have you noticed there are chickens? In Italy you get chickens but no eggs. In Africa there were always eggs, but never chickens. Who separated them?

HANA
(*intrigued*)
You were in Africa?

CARAVAGGIO
Yes, I was.

HANA
So was my Patient.

CARAVAGGIO
Look, I'd like to stay for a while. I have to do some work here – I speak the language. There are Partisans to be disarmed –
(*trying to paraphrase*)
– we embrace them and see if we can relieve them of their weapons, you know – while we

hug. I was a thief, so the Army thought I'd be
good at it.

HANA

So you can shoot a pistol?

CARAVAGGIO
(showing his hands)

No.

HANA

Do you have a problem with those?

CARAVAGGIO

No.

HANA

I should look at them before you go.

CARAVAGGIO

Look, it's a big place. We needn't disturb each
other. I'll sleep in the stable. It doesn't matter
where I sleep. I don't sleep.

HANA

I don't know what Mary told you about me, but I
don't need company, I don't need to be looked
after.

Int. The Patient's room. Day

HANA *carries in a tray. There's omelette on the plate.*

HANA

There's a man downstairs. He brought us eggs.
He might stay.

THE PATIENT
Why? Can he lay eggs?

HANA
He's Canadian.

THE PATIENT
(brittle)
Why are people always so happy when they
collide with someone from the same place?
What happened in Montreal when you passed a
man in the street – did you invite him to live
with you?

HANA
He needn't disturb you.

THE PATIENT
Me? He can't. I'm already disturbed.

HANA
(she cuts the omelette into tiny pieces)
There's a war. Where you come from becomes
important.

THE PATIENT
Why? I hate that idea.

Int. The monastery stairs. Day

CARAVAGGIO is in shadows in the hallway. He listens.

Int. The Patient's room. Day

HANA, having already replaced the bed linen, is standing
on a stepladder trying to hang homemade drapes around

the bed as CARAVAGGIO *knocks tentatively, then comes in.*

CARAVAGGIO

Can I help?

HANA

It's finished.

THE PATIENT

So you're our Canadian pickpocket?

CARAVAGGIO

Thief, I think, is more accurate.

THE PATIENT

I understand you were in Africa. Whereabouts?

CARAVAGGIO

Oh, all over.

THE PATIENT

All over? I kept trying to cover a very modest portion and still failed.
(*to* HANA, *who is heading out*)
Are you leaving us?

HANA

Yes.

THE PATIENT

Now's our opportunity to swap war wounds.

HANA

Then I'm definitely going.

And she exits. The men consider her.

CARAVAGGIO
Does she have war wounds?

Int. The monastery, Hana's room. Day

As HANA walks up her stairs she finds herself overhearing their conversation as it threads up through the hole in the ceiling. She strips her own bed of the curtain she uses for a sheet.

THE PATIENT
I think anybody she ever loves tends to die on her.

CARAVAGGIO
Are you planning to be the exception?

THE PATIENT
Me? I think you've got the wrong end of the stick, old boy.
(a pause)
So, Caravaggio – Hana thinks you invented your name.

CARAVAGGIO
And you've forgotten yours.

THE PATIENT
I said that no one would ever invent such a preposterous name.

CARAVAGGIO
I said you can forget everything but you never forget your name. Count Almásy – that name mean anything to you? Or Katharine Clifton?

Ext. Cairo market. Day

A street market in full sway, a locals-only affair, blazing with noise and bustle and barter. Emerging from a thicket of women and begging children, KATHARINE CLIFTON carries her purchase of an exotic-looking carpet. From nowhere she is joined by ALMÁSY, who nods at the carpet.

ALMÁSY

How much did you pay?

KATHARINE
(*delighted*)

Oh, hello!

ALMÁSY

They don't see foreign women in this market.
How much did you pay?

KATHARINE

Seven, eight pounds, I suppose.

ALMÁSY

Which stall?

KATHARINE

Why?

ALMÁSY

You've been cheated, don't worry, we'll take it back.

KATHARINE
(*bristling*)
I don't want to take it back.

ALMÁSY

This is not worth eight pounds, Mrs Clifton.

KATHARINE

It is to me.

ALMÁSY

Did you bargain?

KATHARINE

I don't care to bargain.

ALMÁSY

That insults them.

KATHARINE
(*turning to face him*)
I don't believe that. I think you are insulted by
me, somehow.

ALMÁSY
(*of the carpet*)
I'd be very happy to obtain the correct price for
this. I apologize if I appear abrupt. I am rusty at
social graces.
(*tart*)
How do you find Cairo? Did you visit the
Pyramids?

KATHARINE

Excuse me.

ALMÁSY

Or the Sphinx?

He stands as she continues, pushing past him, boiling.

Int. Shepheard's Hotel, Cairo. Evening

The Long Bar. The exploration team is drinking at a

table. They are not entirely off-duty – ALMÁSY and MADOX, as ever, ponder the maps.

MADOX
By car? Impossible. If we try and drive north of Kufra by car, we'll leave our bones in the desert.

ALMÁSY
Disagree.

MADOX
You're Hungarian, you always disagree.

GEOFFREY CLIFTON appears.

CLIFTON
Good evening, Gentlemen!

He sits down. MADOX hails the waiter.

D'AGOSTINO
How is your charming wife?

CLIFTON
Marvellous. She's in love with the hotel plumbing. She's either in the swimming pool – she swims for hours, she's a fish, quite incredible – or she's in the bath. Actually, she's just outside.
  (responding to their bewildered expressions)
Chaps Only in the Long Bar.

Ext. Shepheard's Hotel terrace. Night

The explorers, embarrassed, march out onto the terrace. KATHARINE sits, reading, exquisite in her evening clothes. There is dancing inside, and couples walk to and from their tables. MADOX approaches to collect her. KATHARINE

manages to produce a dazzling smile which includes every-
one except ALMÁSY.

MADOX

Mrs Clifton, you'll have to forgive us. We're not
accustomed to the company of women.

KATHARINE

Not at all. I was thoroughly enjoying my book.

CLIFTON

The team is in mourning, darling.

KATHARINE

Oh really?

MADOX

I'm afraid we're not having much luck obtaining
funds for the expedition.

KATHARINE

Oh. What will you do?

MADOX

A more modest expedition, or even wait a year.
Remind our families we still exist.

CLIFTON
(*astonished*)
Good heavens, are you married, Madox?

MADOX

Very much so. We all are, save my friend here.

He nods at ALMÁSY. CLIFTON *appears tremendously*
relieved.

43

CLIFTON

I feel much better, don't you darling? We were
feeling rather self-conscious. Let's toast, then.
To absent wives.

D'AGOSTINO
(*toasting* KATHARINE)
And present ones.

KATHARINE
(*toasting* ALMÁSY)
And future ones.

Int. Shepheard's Hotel. Night

The ballroom. A dance finishes. ALMÁSY *takes over from*
D'AGOSTINO *to partner* KATHARINE. *The others remain
on the terrace, deep in conversation.*

KATHARINE
(*as they dance*)
Why did you follow me yesterday?

ALMÁSY

What? I'm sorry?

KATHARINE
After the market, you followed me to the hotel.

ALMÁSY
I was concerned. A woman in that part of Cairo,
a European woman, I felt obliged to.

KATHARINE
You felt obliged to.

ALMÁSY
As the wife of one of our party.

KATHARINE
(direct)
So why follow me? Escort me, by all means. But
following me is predatory, isn't it?

ALMÁSY, *by way of answer, bears down on her. They
dance, fierce, oblivious to everything.*

Int. The Patient's room. Night

HANA *has fallen asleep on the bed, almost on top of* THE
PATIENT. *He touches her. He speaks as if each word
burns him.*

THE PATIENT
Could I ask you to move? I'm sorry –

HANA
(mortified, moving quickly)
I'm sorry, of course. I was dreaming. Awful.

THE PATIENT
It's just when you move –

HANA
How stupid of me.

THE PATIENT
– I can't really bear the pressure.

HANA *gets up, upset to have hurt him.*

Int. The monastery kitchen. Night

HANA *comes to the table, carrying a jug of water and a*

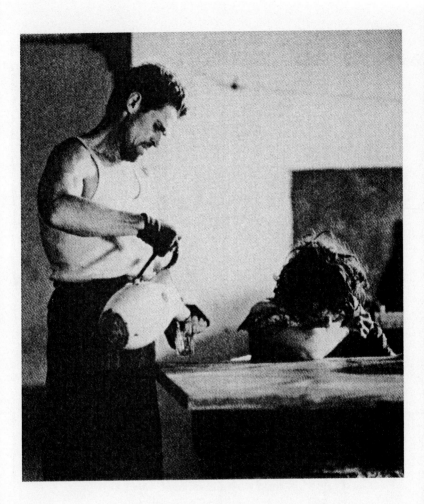

bowl. She's still sad. She unbuttons her dress, pulling it off her shoulder, begins to pour the water to cool herself against the night's pressing heat. She's overwhelmed by memories, by the weight of her curse. CARAVAGGIO *comes into the kitchen to find her slumped at the table, her back naked, the jug of water in front of her. She's sobbing, her shoulders heaving.* CARAVAGGIO *approaches tentatively.*

CARAVAGGIO

Hana?
(*he touches her shoulder*)
Hana? Are you all right?

HANA
(*without raising her head*)
Don't touch me.

She pulls her dress up around her shoulders. Her face is red with weeping. CARAVAGGIO *pours a glass of water and walks to the open window.*

CARAVAGGIO

You're in love with him, aren't you? Your poor
Patient. Do you think he's a saint because of the
way he looks? I don't think he is.

HANA

I'm not in love with him. I'm in love with
ghosts. So is he. He's in love with ghosts.

CARAVAGGIO
(*he holds up his hands*)
What if I told you he did this to me?

HANA
(*stung*)
How could he have? When?

CARAVAGGIO

I'm one of his ghosts and he wouldn't even know
it.

HANA

I don't know what that means.

CARAVAGGIO
(*shrugs*)
Ask your saint who he is. Ask him who he's
killed.

HANA
(*furious*)
Please don't creep around this house!

She leaves, slamming the door behind her. CARAVAGGIO
calls after her.

CARAVAGGIO

I don't think he's forgotten anything. I think he
wants to forget.

Int. Tent, Base Camp at Pottery Hill. Night

The group of expeditioners is around the fire. CLIFTON
holds up a glass.

CLIFTON
Gentlemen, to map-making!

ALL
Map-making!

MADOX
And a special thank-you to Geoffrey and

Katharine, without whose fund-raising heroics
we'd still be kicking our heels.

CLIFTON

To arm-twisting.

MADOX
(*to* ALMÁSY)
Did Katharine say? Geoffrey has to fly back to
Cairo.

CLIFTON

Return the favour – take a few photographs of
the Army.

ALMÁSY

What kind of photographs?

CLIFTON

Portraits. The Brigadier, the Brigadier's wife,
the Brigadier's dogs, the Brigadier by the
Pyramids, the Brigadier breathing. I shall of
course be bereft, but finally able to explore the
Cairo nightlife. I shall produce an authoritative
guide to the Zinc Bars and – I want to say
Harems – are we in the right country for
Harems?

Ext. Base Camp at Pottery Hill. Morning

As CLIFTON *prepares to leave in the Steerman,* ALMÁSY
approaches.

ALMÁSY

Clifton, safe journey.

CLIFTON

You too. Good luck!

ALMÁSY

Clifton – it's probably none of my business – but
your wife, do you think it's appropriate to leave
her?

CLIFTON

Appropriate?

ALMÁSY

Well, the desert is – for a woman – it's very
tough, I wonder if it's not too much for her.

CLIFTON

Are you mad? Katharine loves it here. She told
me yesterday.

ALMÁSY

All the same, were I you, I would be
concerned –

CLIFTON

I've known Katharine since she was three, we
were practically brother and sister before we
were man and wife. I think I'd know what is and
what isn't too much for her. I think she'd know
herself.

ALMÁSY

Very well.

CLIFTON
(laughing it off)
Why are you people so threatened by a woman?!

ALMÁSY *watches him walk toward the plane, then turns to see* KATHARINE, *a distant figure, watching. He doesn't move. She doesn't move.*

Int. Monastery library. Day

HANA *stands at the piano. It's still lopsided, propped against the wall. She tries but can't move it. So she pulls off the dust sheet and, with the instrument on a tilt, begins to pick out the Aria from Bach's* Goldberg Variations.

Int. The Patient's room. Day

HANA's *piano continues. Upstairs,* CARAVAGGIO *chats with* THE PATIENT *while working his arm to raise a vein, a bootlace tied around it, preparing an injection for himself, tapping the syringe. During this:*

THE PATIENT
I have come to love that little tap of the fingernail against the syringe. Tap. Tap. Tap.

Int. Monastery library. Day

HANA *plays. A gunshot punctuates the music. Her hands falter, she looks up to see a Sikh soldier running past the gaping hole in the wall, his rifle held aloft. He approaches the French doors, his face creased with anxiety, and raps on the shattered frame. It's* KIP, *the bomb disposal officer who had cleared the road on which* JAN's *jeep had exploded.*

KIP
Stop playing! Please, stop playing!

HANA
(of the doors)
I don't have the key to that door.

She watches him walk around from the locked doors and walk straight through the hole in the wall, oblivious to any irony, and up to the piano.

KIP

The Germans were here. The Germans were all over this area. They left mines everywhere. And pianos were their favourite hiding places.

HANA

I see. Sorry.
(*then mischievous*)
Then maybe you're safe as long as you only play Bach. He's German.

Kip is looking around the piano. Hana giggles.

KIP

Is something funny?

HANA

No, I'm sorry.

KIP

I've met you before.

HANA

I don't think so.

KIP

Look. See. See.

Hana bends to see what Kip's looking at under the piano. Wires run from the wall to the instrument onto which is taped an explosive charge. If Hana had succeeded in moving the piano she would have triggered the charge. Kip looks at Hana, who conceals her dismay with a shrug.

KIP
(*of the piano*)
Move that, and no more Bach.

Ext. The monastery garden. Dusk

Across from the terrace, KIP and his sergeant, HARDY, are putting up their tents. CARAVAGGIO stands, chatting amiably to them, holding a haversack, smoking a cigarette.

Int. The Patient's room. Dusk

HANA looks down from THE PATIENT's room, watching the tent go up. KIP glances up at the window. HANA, suddenly shy, backs away.

HANA
He wants us to move out, says there could be fifty more mines in the building. He thinks I'm mad because I laughed at him. He's Indian, he wears a turban.

THE PATIENT
No, he's Sikh. If he wears a turban, he's Sikh.

HANA
I'll probably marry him.

THE PATIENT
Really? That's sudden.

HANA
My mother always told me I would summon my husband by playing the piano.

She bathes THE PATIENT.

HANA

I liked it better when there were just the two of us.

THE PATIENT
(*irked*)
Why? Is he staying?

HANA
With his Sergeant. A Mr Hardy.

THE PATIENT
We should charge! Doesn't anyone have a job to do?

HANA
They have to clear all the roads of mines. That's a big job.

THE PATIENT
In that case, I suppose we can't charge.

HANA
No, we can't.

Ext. The monastery, Hana's garden. Day

HANA *is gardening, close to the crucifix, which is now a full-fledged scarecrow. Broken bottles, fragments of stained glass, and shards from a mirror are hung from the crossbar, syringes too, all jangling and tinkling and catching the sunlight.*

KIP *and* HARDY *drive off to work on their motorcycles. She watches them, catching* KIP's *careless wave to her. She looks briefly at herself in a piece of mirror dangling from the scarecrow.*

Int. The Patient's room. Day

THE PATIENT *lies in bed singing to himself in Arabic.*

Ext. Base Camp at Pottery Hill

The three Ford cars leave the campsite, loaded for a scouting expedition. The rest of the party – Bedouin, tents, camels, and Tiger Moth – is left behind.

Int. Car en route to Cave of Swimmers. Day

ALMÁSY drives the second car, accompanied by KATHAR-INE and AL AUF, who sits on top of the cabin. ALMÁSY sings as they drive. KATHARINE breaks the long silence between them.

KATHARINE
I've been thinking – how does somebody like
you decide to come to the desert? What is it?
You're doing whatever you're doing – in your
castle, or wherever it is you live – and one day
you say *I have to go to the desert* – or what?

ALMÁSY doesn't answer. KATHARINE, who has looked at him for an answer, looks away. There's another long silence.

ALMÁSY
I once travelled with a guide, who was taking me
to Faya. He didn't speak for nine hours. At the
end of it he pointed at the horizon and said,
'Faya!' That was a good day.

Point made, they lapse again into silence. KATHARINE boils.

57

                    KATHARINE
Actually, you sing.

                    ALMÁSY
What?

                    KATHARINE
You sing. All the time.

                    ALMÁSY
I do not.

                    KATHARINE
Ask Al Auf.

*In Arabic, ALMÁSY asks AL AUF, who promptly laughs,
nods, and sings a snatch of what he thinks is the tune to
'The Darktown Strutter's Ball'. KATHARINE, delighted,
joins in.*

                    KATHARINE
                 (*sings wickedly*)
*I'll be down to get you in the taxi, honey, you'd
better be ready about half-past eight . . .*

*AL AUF nods and grins furiously, joins in, impersonating
ALMÁSY. ALMÁSY makes a face.*

Ext. Near the Base Camp at the Cave of Swimmers. Dusk

*The group is investigating a cleft in the rocky massif. They
climb slowly. Below them, a new and temporary base camp.*

*The group winds around the rock. ALMÁSY turns to offer
a hand to KATHARINE behind him, pulling her up to the
next rock slab.*

The group stops at a level plateau. The Arabs stand apart and sing their prayers at dusk. AL AUF leads the incantations.

AL AUF
Allah Akbar, Allahu Akbar . . .

The Westerners wait respectfully. As the sun sets in glory, ALMÁSY looks over at the range of rocks. One particular range seems to look exactly like a woman's back. He squints at the rocks, then pulls out his Herodotus to compare his sketch map with the terrain in front of him.

Ext. Cave of Swimmers. Dusk

ALMÁSY clambers up the rocks, coming through a narrow crevice to find a natural shelf. He scrambles up this path, reaching up, only to notice that his hand almost perfectly covers a carved hand on the rock, and as he digests this he realizes he has climbed past what is the mouth of a cave. He disappears inside.

Int. Cave of Swimmers. Flashlight

A flashlight squirts into the cave. ALMÁSY treads cautiously along the narrow winding passage. He comes to an open cavern and takes his flashlight up to a wall. ALMÁSY is astonished by what he sees.

Ext. Near the Cave of Swimmers. Evening

The others watch as a flashlight bobs and jerks among the rocks and ALMÁSY comes scrambling down, transformed into an excited teenager.

ALMÁSY
Madox! Madox! Madox, come quickly!
Bermann, D'Ag – I've found something.

Int. Cave of Swimmers. Flashlight

Paintings emerge, figures, animals. Ancient pictures. A giraffe. Cattle. Fish. Men with bows and arrows. ALMÁSY has led the whole party into the heart of the cave. Now MADOX comes alongside him at the wall, his flashlight joining ALMÁSY's and increasing the visibility of the paintings. A dark-skinned figure, apparently in the process of diving into water, comes clearly into view. Then others, supine, arms outstretched.

MADOX
(with audible excitement)

My God, they're swimming! They're swimming!

The others crowd around. Five excited faces in the green gloom of the cave.

Int. Cave of Swimmers. Day

KATHARINE *is painting. She copies the cave paintings with meticulous, almost scientific accuracy.*

Ext. Cave of Swimmers. Day

A hive of activity. The team has set up trestles to catalogue the finds as the Bedouin come out with baskets of detritus, which they empty onto a growing heap as the cave is cleared out. ALMÁSY *clambers inside carrying camera equipment.*

Int. Cave of Swimmers. Day

Inside, BERMANN *is setting up lamps, running wires from a car battery.* KAMAL *is helping him. And as* ALMÁSY *arrives he catches a tiny moment of tenderness between them.* BERMANN, *seeing him, quickly disengages and busies himself with the lights.*

Ext. The desert. Day

The cars are heading back to Base Camp. They bounce over the sand.

Int. Bermann's car. Day

BERMANN *is driving the lead car along some steep dunes.* ALMÁSY *beside him.* BERMANN *is peeling an orange, a segment of which he holds out of the window.* KAMAL, *riding shotgun, leans down and collects it, his head dipping in to grin at* BERMANN. BERMANN *looks uneasily at* ALMÁSY. *He wants to tell him of his passion, of his absolute love for* KAMAL, *but he daren't.*

> BERMANN
> How do you explain? To someone who's never been here? Feelings which seem quite normal.

ALMÁSY
(compassionate)
I don't know, my friend. I don't know.

BERMANN *holds out another segment of the orange, and watches* KAMAL *bend into view, opening his mouth to be fed another piece, then suddenly fall from the vehicle. The car lurches sideways and topples over the edge.* D'AG – *following,* FOUAD *beside him – brakes sharply, but can't stop his own car from being caught in the avalanche of sand, and it plunges down the dune and into* BERMANN's *upturned car with an ominous crunch, the radiator exploding. Only* MADOX, *a little way behind, with* KATHARINE *beside him, manages to stay clear of trouble. He jumps out of the vehicle and slides down the dune to find pandemonium as the passengers stumble out of the cars, sand flying, smoke pouring from the upright vehicle, the wheels of the overturned car spinning wildly in the air, a puddle of oil spreading ominously.*

Ext. The desert. Day

Later and the group have cleaned up as best as possible. D'AG, BERMANN, *and* FOUAD *are a little worse for wear.* FOUAD's *arm is in a sling, and* D'AG *is sporting a bloody head bandage.* BERMANN *has broken a finger and is being attended to by* MADOX. *The luggage, water, and petrol have been stacked up and the men are loading the remaining car.*

Ext. The desert. Day

ALMÁSY, KAMAL, *and two of the other young Bedouin stand around the mess of the two broken vehicles. The one working car is loaded with men and provisions.*

KATHARINE *sits inside, next to* MADOX. ALMÁSY *comes over to her window, to speak past her to* MADOX.

MADOX

I'll be back as quick as I can. Thirty-six hours at the outside.

ALMÁSY

Try to get an additional radiator. We can store it between here and Pottery Hill. And a better jack. We planned badly.

MADOX
(*nods at* ALMÁSY, *then shouts over to the wrecked vehicles*)

Bermann!

This is BERMANN'S *cue to take leave of* KAMAL, *who is staying behind.* KAMAL *makes a little bow.*

KAMAL
(*in Arabic*)

May God make safety your companion.

BERMANN *nods and hurries away, squeezing into the car, which jolts off, bouncing over the track.*

The vehicle gets about twenty yards, ALMÁSY *watching, before it sinks forlornly into the soft sand. It's hopelessly overloaded with people. They all get out.*

MADOX
(*irascible*)

Now what?

KATHARINE

I'll stay behind, of course.

MADOX

Certainly not.

KATHARINE

No, I insist. There clearly isn't room for all of us,
I'm the least able to dig, and I'm not one of the
walking wounded. It's only one night! Besides, if
I remain it's the most effective method of
persuading my husband to abandon whatever
he's doing and come and rescue us.

It's hard to argue with this logic. ALMÁSY *shrugs.*

Later – the MADOX *car makes a more effective departure.*
ALMÁSY *watches it disappear then turns, uncomfortable,
to see* KATHARINE *walk down the steep face of the dune
toward the makeshift shelter.*

Int. Shelter. Day

ALMÁSY *sits alone, writing into his* Herodotus, *a map
folded in front of him, from which he makes notes.*
KATHARINE *comes across with a clutch of her sketches
from the cave wall. Hands them to him. They're
beautiful.*

KATHARINE

I thought you might like to paste them into your
book.

ALMÁSY

Well, we took photographs, there's no need.

KATHARINE

No really, I'd like you to have them.

ALMÁSY
(*handing them back*)
Well, there is really no need. They're too good.
This is just a scrapbook. I should feel obliged.
Thank you.

KATHARINE
(*exasperated*)
And that would be unconscionable, I suppose,
wouldn't it, to feel any obligation? Yes. Of
course it would.

*She's already turning, heading back up the slope, leaving
the perimeter of the shelter.*

Ext. The desert. Night

KATHARINE *sits alone on top of the dune, smoking,
surveying the landscape. Below her the camp – a fresh
wind flicking at the tarpaulin, the deep tracks of* MADOX's
car stretching off toward civilization. ALMÁSY *heads up
toward her.*

ALMÁSY
You should come into the shelter.

KATHARINE
I'm quite all right, thank you.

ALMÁSY
Look over there.

KATHARINE *turns, scans the horizon.*

KATHARINE
What am I looking at?

ALMÁSY

Do you see what's happening to them – the stars?

KATHARINE

They're so untidy. I'm just trying to rearrange them.

ALMÁSY

No, no, over there. In a few minutes there will be no stars. The air is filling with sand.

On the distant dunes an ominous, boiling cloud.

Ext. Vehicles. Night

The team hurries around salvaging gasoline drums, water cans, bringing anything loose or light inside the vehicles. The wind is whipping up, the air busy with sand. Chaos as they struggle in ever-worsening conditions, their heads wrapped in blankets, flashlights useless. They seek safety in two groups, the tribesmen to the cabin of the overturned car, KATHARINE and ALMÁSY to the upright one.

Int. Car. Night

Inside the cabin, the sand swirling around them, KATHARINE and ALMÁSY sit without speaking. He pours a little water so that they can wash out their eyes and noses and mouths. She takes her silk scarf, wets it, presses it to her face.

KATHARINE

This is not very good, is it?

ALMÁSY

No.

67

KATHARINE
Shall we be all right?

ALMÁSY
Yes. Yes. Absolutely.

KATHARINE
Yes is a comfort. *Absolutely* is not.

Ext. The desert. Night

The sand is piling up against the two cars, the tent is swept from its moorings, the water cans are hurled up, too, and then plunge ominously into sand drifts as if going under an ocean.

ALMÁSY (o/s)
. . . let me tell you about winds. There is a whirlwind from Southern Morocco, the *Aajej*, against which the fellahin defend themselves with knives. And there is the *Ghibli* from Tunis which rolls and rolls and rolls and produces a rather strange nervous condition . . .

And we hear KATHARINE's laugh.

Int. Car. Night

ALMÁSY sits alongside KATHARINE, whose head is against his shoulder. He continues his story of winds.

ALMÁSY
. . . and then there is the *Harmatton*, a red wind which mariners call the sea of darkness. Red sand from this wind has flown as far as the south coast of England apparently producing showers so dense they were mistaken for blood . . .

KATHARINE

Fiction. We have a house on that coast, and it
has never, never rained blood.

ALMÁSY

No, it's all true.
(*teasing her*)
Herodotus, your friend –

KATHARINE
(*laughs*)

My friend!

ALMÁSY

– he writes about it and he writes about a wind,
the *Simoon*, which a nation thought was so evil
they declared war on it and marched out against
it in full battle dress.

He's touching KATHARINE's *hair, he can't help it. She is
paralyzed by his touch, then puts out her hand and traces
across the window, now entirely silted up with sand.*

Int. Patient's room. Night

THE PATIENT *remembers. He feels* KATHARINE's *fingers
tracing across his face.*

Ext. The desert. Day

*Morning. The sand has almost completely engulfed the car
on the exposed side, covering the windscreen like snow,
and encroaching onto the door of the protected flank.*

Int. Car. Day

ALMÁSY *is awakened by the sound of a distant engine. He*

jerks up, waking KATHARINE *in the process, and heaves against the door.*

ALMÁSY

Quick. Katharine. Quick, wake up! I can hear a car. Let me out.
> (*he stumbles out of the car, up the dune,
> then stops and flies back to the car*)

The flare!
> (*berating himself*)

Idiot! To fall asleep. Unforgiveable.

Ext. The desert. Day

MADOX's *car is roaring along the horizon.* ALMÁSY *runs back into the car, finds his flaregun, and sends a flare high into the sky.* KATHARINE *is with him now, and they watch, helplessly, as the car bounces away from them,* MADOX *a man on a mission.* KATHARINE *panics, the sand has erased all trace of them.* KATHARINE *waves her arms frantically.*

KATHARINE

Here! We're here! Stop!

ALMÁSY

Madox! Madox!

KATHARINE

Our tracks have disappeared.

ALMÁSY

Madox will calculate how many miles; he'll soon turn around.

KATHARINE *is frightened. He looks at her.*

ALMÁSY

Could I ask you, please, to paste your paintings
into my book? I should like to have them. I
should be honoured.

*A car horn leaks into their conversation. ALMÁSY can't
place it at first – he'd assumed it was MADOX. Now he
realizes it's coming from the floor of the sand dune. He
suddenly turns and charges away from KATHARINE.*

ALMÁSY

The others!

*KATHARINE, horrified, follows him toward the mound of
sand which has completely buried the other vehicle.*

KATHARINE

Awful. We must get them out! How awful.

*ALMÁSY is preoccupied. He's gone back to their vehicle
and returns with a shovel, starts to dig frantically.
KATHARINE kneels beside him and helps to shovel away
the sand. During this:*

KATHARINE

Am I a terrible coward to ask how much water
we have?

ALMÁSY
(shovelling hard)

We have a little in our can, we have water in
the radiator which can be drunk. It's not
cowardly at all, it's extremely practical.
    (anxious at not uncovering the boys,
      egging himself on)
Come on, come one!
    (then back to KATHARINE)

There's also a plant – I believe you can cut a
piece the size of a heart from this plant and the
next morning it will be filled with a delicious
liquid.

KATHARINE
Find that plant. Cut out its heart.

*They hear noises, scrabbling, faint thumps. ALMÁSY
scrapes at the sand and they find the glass of the car. The
angle of the cab, tilted up to the sky, has made it
impossible for the trapped boys to lever it open. Their
oxygen is rapidly deteriorating. ALMÁSY pulls on the door
and it cranks open. The boys, dazed, gulping in the fresh
air, clamber out.*

Ext. The desert. Day

*KATHARINE sits in the car, putting her pictures into the
Herodotus. It's full of ALMÁSY's handwriting, photographs, some pressed flowers. She deciphers a page of his
words and drawings. It's almost exclusively about her, the
lines studded with Ks. She reads, astonished, then looks at
him as he and two of the three Bedouin circle the area of
the cars in ever-widening circles, like water-diviners, like
KIP searching for mines. ALMÁSY suddenly drops to his
knees and begins to shovel into the sand. He pulls out a
can of water. Turns to KATHARINE and holds it
triumphantly in the air.*

Int. The desert. Night

*A red umbrella of light as ALMÁSY fires the last flare into
the black night. KATHARINE comes up beside him. They
wait in silence, hope fading with the flare.*

KATHARINE
(blank)
Geoffrey's not in Cairo.
(ALMÁSY looks at her)
He's not actually a buffoon. And the plane
wasn't a wedding present. It belongs to the
British Government. They want aerial maps of
the whole of North Africa. So I think he's in
Ethiopia. In case you were counting on his
sudden appearance.

ALMÁSY
And the marriage – is that a fiction?

There's a beat. KATHARINE *has a hundred answers.*

KATHARINE
No, the marriage isn't a fiction.

*The light from the flare fades on them and they stand in
the dark. Suddenly on the far horizon, behind their heads,
an answering flare fireworks into the sky.*

KATHARINE
Thank God. Oh thank God.

*There's excited shouting from the boys. Then a distant
reply.* ALMÁSY *laughs with relief.*

ALMÁSY
It's Madox.

He turns to KATHARINE. *She shudders.*

KATHARINE
Am I K in your book? I think I must be.

ALMÁSY *turns to her. He runs the blade of his arm across her neck.*

Int. The monastery, upstairs landing. Day

HANA *walks along the landing with a tray. There's a message on several doors in the corridor from* KIP: SAFE, *then a couple with the warning:* DANGER. *She hears noise from* THE PATIENT's *room. Listens for a second before going in.* KIP *is reading to* THE PATIENT.

KIP (o/s)
(*reading*)
'He sat, in defiance of municipal orders, astride the gun Zamzammah on her brick platform opposite the old Ajaib-Gher – '
(*he breaks off*)
I can't read these words. They stick in my throat.

THE PATIENT (o/s)
Because you're reading it too fast!

KIP (o/s)
Not at all.

THE PATIENT (o/s)
You have to read Kipling slowly! Your eye is too impatient – think about the speed of his pen.
(*quoting Kipling to demonstrate*)
What is it? 'He sat' *comma* 'in defiance of municipal orders' *comma* 'astride the gun Zamzammah on her brick' . . . what is it?

Int. The Patient's room. Day

During this, HANA *comes through with the tray, finds* KIP *perched on the window, relishing his skirmish with* THE

PATIENT, *who has condensed milk dribbling down his neck.*

KIP

'Brick platform opposite the old Ajaib-Gher – '

THE PATIENT

' – The Wonder House' *comma* 'as the natives called the Lahore Museum.'

KIP

It's still there, the cannon, outside the museum. It was made of metal cups and bowls taken from every household in the city as tax, then melted down. Then later they fired the cannon at my people *comma* the natives. *Full stop.*

THE PATIENT

So what is it you object to – the writer or what he's writing about?

KIP

What I really object to, Uncle, is your finishing all my condensed milk.
    (*snatching up the empty can*)
And the message everywhere in your book – however slowly I read it – that the best destiny for India is to be ruled by the British.

THE PATIENT

Hana, we have discovered a shared pleasure – the boy and I.

HANA

Arguing about books.

THE PATIENT
Condensed milk – one of the truly great
inventions.

KIP
(grinning, leaving)
I'll get another tin.

HANA and THE PATIENT are alone.

HANA
I didn't like that book either. It's all about men.
Too many men. Just like this house.

THE PATIENT
You like him, don't you? Your voice changes.

HANA
I don't think it does.
(a beat)
Anyway, he's indifferent to me.

THE PATIENT
I don't think it's indifference.

KIP comes bounding in with a fresh can.

THE PATIENT
Hana was just telling me you were indifferent –

HANA
(appalled)
Hey!

THE PATIENT
– to her cooking.

KIP
(*oblivious*)
Well, I'm indifferent to cooking, not Hana's
cooking in particular.
(*stabbing at the tin with a bayonet*)
Have either of you ever tried condensed milk
sandwiches?

Ext. Cairo. Day

Another world as a honking taxi containing ALMÁSY *and*
KATHARINE *negotiates the pell-mell bustle of Ciro.*

Ext. Shepheard's Hotel. Day

ALMÁSY, *still in the same clothes, and evidently weary,
emerges from the cab, and pulls* KATHARINE'S *belongings
from the trunk, then holds open the door for her. As she
walks toward the hotel, he hands her bag to a porter.*
KATHARINE *is stung.*

KATHARINE
Will you not come in?

ALMÁSY
No. I should go home.

KATHARINE
Will you please come in?

ALMÁSY
(*a beat*)
Mrs Clifton –

KATHARINE *turns, disgusted.*

KATHARINE

Don't.

ALMÁSY

I believe you still have my book.

KATHARINE *fishes the book from her knapsack, shoves it at him, then disappears inside the hotel.*

Int. Almásy's room. Day

ALMÁSY *lying on a camp bed, face down. The walls are covered with maps, enlargements of photographs. A fan whirs over his kit which is spread, unravelled but ordered, on the stone floor. An ineffably male room, the shutters closed, just the thinnest shaft of light piercing the gloom. ALMÁSY hasn't even removed his clothes, his boots kicked off below his jutting feet.*

There's a knock at the door. ALMÁSY *sleeps. Another. A third. He's roused from the dead.*

It's KATHARINE. *She's bathed, luminous, stands backlit by the afternoon sun – an angel in a cotton dress. He walks toward her and she* **slaps** *him, shockingly hard. He kneels before her, head at her thighs.* KATHARINE *beats on his head and shoulders, violently, then stops, her face expressionless.*

KATHARINE

You still have sand in your hair.

He pulls back, to look at her. She kneels and covers his face with kisses. He pulls blindly at her dress and it rips across her breasts.

Int. Bathroom. Day

ALMÁSY *is in the bath.* KATHARINE, *wearing his dressing gown, pours in a jug of steaming water.* ALMÁSY *leans over the rim of the bath. He's singing and sewing, carefully repairing the torn dress.*

KATHARINE
I'm impressed you can sew.

ALMÁSY
Good.

KATHARINE
You sew very badly.

ALMÁSY
You don't sew at all!

KATHARINE
A woman should never learn to sew, and if she can she shouldn't admit to it. Close your eyes.

ALMÁSY
(*laughs*)
That makes it harder still.

She pushes the sewing from his hands, then pours water over his head, begins to shampoo his hair.

ALMÁSY *is in heaven. The biggest smile we have seen from him. She continues to massage his scalp.*

ALMÁSY
When were you most happy?

KATHARINE
Now.

ALMÁSY
When were you least happy?

KATHARINE
(a beat)
Now.

ALMÁSY
What do you love?

KATHARINE
What do I love?

ALMÁSY
Say everything.

KATHARINE
Let me see . . . I love water, the fish in it.
Hedgehogs! I love hedgehogs.

She rinses his hair, then slips off the robe and climbs in beside him, covering his neck and shoulders in kisses.

ALMÁSY
And what else?

KATHARINE
Marmite – I'm addicted! Baths – but not with
other people! Islands. Your handwriting. I could
go on all day.

ALMÁSY
(kissing her)
Go on all day.

KATHARINE
(a beat)
My husband.

ALMÁSY *looks away.*

> ALMÁSY
> What do you hate most?

> KATHARINE
> A lie. What do you hate most?

> ALMÁSY
> Ownership. Being owned. When you leave, you
> should forget me.

*She freezes, pushes him away, pulls herself out of the bath.
She picks up her dress, the thread and needle dangling from
it, and walks, dripping, out of the room.*

Int. The Patient's room. Day

HANA *sits reading from the* Herodotus. *She pulls out a
photograph of a small child.*

> HANA
> Who is this?

> THE PATIENT
> Don't you recognize me?

> HANA
> (*laughs*)
> Is it you? So fat!

Next she shows THE PATIENT *the page where a
Christmas cracker wrapper covered in handwriting has
been glued in.*

> THE PATIENT
> That's a Christmas cracker. It was a Christmas
> cracker. A firecracker.

HANA

This isn't your handwriting, is it?

THE PATIENT

Yes, it is.

HANA
(she reads what he's written)

'December twenty-second – Betrayals in war are
childlike compared with our betrayals during
peace. New lovers are nervous and tender, but
smash everything – for the heart is an organ of
fire . . . for the heart is an organ of fire . . .'
(she looks up)
I love that, I believe that.
(to him)
K. Who is K?

THE PATIENT

K is for Katharine.

Ext. Ambassador's residence, December 1938. Day

*A Christmas party for the troops. The incongruous
attempts to create a traditional Christmas in the dusty heat
of Cairo. The party is in the courtyard of the Moorish
Palace, which serves as the private residence of the British
Ambassador, SIR RONNIE HAMPTON. Lots of wives, in-
cluding LADY HAMPTON and KATHARINE, help serve tea
and cake to the soldiers who sit at rudimentary tables with
paper plates and paper hats. A man dressed as Santa
Claus is giving out presents – Penguin paperbacks,
chocolate. Christmas carols leak from a loudspeaker.
Officers and Civilians walk the perimeter. One of these,
arriving, is ALMÁSY. He sits in the shade, catches
KATHARINE's attention. KATHARINE brings him over a
cup of tea and a plate with Christmas cake on it.*

ALMÁSY

Say you're sick.

KATHARINE

What? No!

ALMÁSY

Say you're feeling faint – the heat.

KATHARINE
(*but a frisson*)

No.

ALMÁSY

I can't work. I can't sleep.

LADY HAMPTON *calls impatiently.*

LADY HAMPTON

Katharine!

KATHARINE

Coming.
(*to* ALMÁSY)

I can't sleep. I woke up shouting in the middle of
the night. Geoffrey thinks it's the thing in the
desert, the trauma.

ALMÁSY

I can still taste you.

KATHARINE
(*waving at another woman who pushes a
trolley with teapots*)

Philippa, this is empty.

ALMÁSY

I'm trying to write with your taste in my mouth.
(*as she leaves*)
Swoon. I'll catch you.

ALMÁSY *sits watching the party. The Santa Claus is dragged outside by some excited children.* ALMÁSY *picks at his cake, removing the thick marzipan icing. He's writing on a Christmas cracker wrapper, smoothing it out –* 'December 22nd. Betrayals in war are childlike compared with our betrayals du – '

KATHARINE, *attending to a table, suddenly sags at the knees, and swoons. People rush to her.*

LADY HAMPTON

Katharine!

KATHARINE

I'm fine. No, I'm fine. How silly.

OFFICER'S WIFE
(*helping her to sit down*)
It's the heat.

LADY HAMPTON
(*to the others*)
She's quite all right.
(*solicitous*)
Are you pregnant?

KATHARINE

I don't think so.

LADY HAMPTON
(*squeezing her arm*)
How romantic. With Fiona I fell over every five minutes. Ronnie christened me Lady Downfall.

84

KATHARINE

Do you know, I think I might go inside and sit down for a few minutes.

LADY HAMPTON

I'll come with you.

KATHARINE

No, please. You stay. I shall be absolutely fine.

Int. Storeroom, Ambassador's residence. Day

A small storeroom inside the Palace – brooms, mops, cleaning equipment. Outside, the party is visible as opaque shadows through the bevelled glass of the ornate window. The sound of carols sung by the enlisted men gives way to a version of 'Silent Night' played on a solitary bagpipe. Inside, ALMÁSY and KATHARINE make love in the darkness. It's as if the world has stopped and there's only their passion, overwhelming reason and logic and rules.

Int. Corridors, Ambassador's residence. Day

A corridor. ALMÁSY appears and almost immediately collides with the man dressed as Santa Claus.

CLIFTON

Have you seen Katharine?

ALMÁSY
(*taken aback*)

What?

CLIFTON
(*pulling down his beard*)

It's Clifton under here.

ALMÁSY
Oh, no, I haven't, sorry.

Int. Side room in ambassador's residence. Day

GEOFFREY *continues scouring the warren of tiny rooms that run off the central courtyard. He finds* KATHARINE *sitting in one, smoking, surrounded by oppressive and elaborate tiling.* CLIFTON *wonders briefly how* ALMÁSY *had missed* KATHARINE.

CLIFTON
Darling, I just heard. You poor sausage, are you all right?

KATHARINE
I'm fine. I'm just hot.

CLIFTON
Lady H said she thought you might be pregnant.

KATHARINE
I'm not pregnant. I'm just hot. Too hot. Aren't you?

CLIFTON
I'm sweltering, actually.
          (*taking off his hat and beard*)
Come on, I'll take you home.

KATHARINE
(*close to tears*)
Can't we really go *home*? I can't breathe. Aren't you dying for green, anything green, or rain. It's Christmas and it's all – oh, I don't know – if you asked me I'd go home tomorrow. If you wanted.

CLIFTON

Darling, you know we can't go home, there
might be a war.

KATHARINE
(*poking at his costume*)
Oh, Geoffrey, you do so love a disguise.

CLIFTON

I do so love you.
                (*he kisses her head*)
What do you smell of?

KATHARINE
(*horrified*)
What?

CLIFTON

Marzipan! I think you've got marzipan in your
hair. No wonder you're homesick.

Int. The Patient's room. Evening

THE PATIENT *lies alone in his room. Then something
distracts him.* CARAVAGGIO *is standing over him, staring,
intense.*

CARAVAGGIO

Is it you?

THE PATIENT

What?

CARAVAGGIO

If I said Moose.

THE PATIENT

Moose? Who the hell's Moose?

CARAVAGGIO *comes close, scrutinizing the face, trying to
repair the features. Exasperated.*

CARAVAGGIO

I look different, why shouldn't you?

THE PATIENT

I heard your breathing, I thought it was the rain.
I'm dying for rain. I'm dying anyway, but I long
for the rain on my face.

CARAVAGGIO
(*a different tack*)

First wedding anniversary – what do you call it?

THE PATIENT

I don't know. Paper. Is it?
          (*sharp, not wanting to think*)
I don't know. Paper.

Int. Office, British HQ, Cairo. Day

*A small office, shared by two men, and a mountain of
filing cabinets and paper. There are aerial maps all over
the walls.* CLIFTON *is on the telephone, while his
colleague,* RUPERT DOUGLAS, *works at the desk.*

CLIFTON
(*into the phone*)

Darling, it's me, I'm sorry, something's come up.

KATHARINE (o/s)

Oh no.

CLIFTON

Don't sulk – I'll be back tomorrow evening. I
promise.

KATHARINE (o/s)

I'm going to sulk. I'm going to sit here and sulk
until you get back.

CLIFTON
(*pleased*)

Good. Okay my sausage, I love you.

RUPERT *makes a face at his friend's sentimentality.*
CLIFTON *beams.*

RUPERT

I didn't know you were going anywhere?

CLIFTON

I'm not. I'm going to surprise her. It's our
anniversary. She's forgotten, of course. What's
the symbol of your first anniversary? I should get
something. Is it cotton or paper?

RUPERT

First anniversary? I thought you two had been
married for donkey's years.

CLIFTON

We've been friends for donkey's years. Best
friends. She was always crying on my shoulder
about somebody – until I persuaded her to settle
for my shoulder. Stroke of genius.
(*he calls through the partition into the next office*)
Moose, you there? First anniversary – is that
cotton?

A man walks into the office, his code name is Moose. We know him as CARAVAGGIO. *He has fewer grey hairs, and thumbs.*

> CARAVAGGIO

Is what cotton?

> CLIFTON

First wedding anniversary.

> CARAVAGGIO

Your first anniversary is Paper.

Ext. Cairo street, o/s Shepheard's Hotel. Day

The approach to the Shepheard's Hotel. GEOFFREY CLIFTON *in a taxi, champagne between his knees.*

The car ahead of them screeches to a halt as a woman hurries across the street. The driver honks his horn angrily. The woman puts up a hand in apology as she skips across the street to another taxi. It's KATHARINE — *she asks the driver for an address in the old town.*

GEOFFREY, *at first excited, is troubled by* KATHARINE'S *expression. Then he sees her skip and his whole being punctures.*

KATHARINE'S *cab roars off. His own car jerks forward.*

> CLIFTON

Stop! Stop here.

> CABBIE

Please? Yessir.

GEOFFREY *sits in the cab. Fifty yards short of the hotel.*
The world rushes by.

Int. Almásy's rooms. Late day

KATHARINE *is in bed.* ALMÁSY *has just put a record on.*
It's the folk song heard at the beginning of the film. He slips
back under the covers. Their clothes are scattered around
the room. He lies over a happy KATHARINE. *She listens.*

KATHARINE
This is – what is this?

ALMÁSY
It's a folk song.

KATHARINE
Arabic?

ALMÁSY
No, no, it's Hungarian. My *daijka* sang it to me
when I was a child in Budapest.

KATHARINE
(*as they listen*)
It's beautiful. What's it about?

ALMÁSY
(*as if interpreting*)
Szerelem means love . . . and the story – there's
this Hungarian count, he's a wanderer, a fool.
For years he's on some kind of a quest, for – who
knows what? And then one day he falls under
the spell of a mysterious English woman – a
harpy – who beats him and hits him and he
becomes her slave and sews her clothes and
worships the hem of her –

KATHARINE *had thought for a few seconds he was serious,
then she catches on and starts to beat him.*

ALMÁSY
(*laughing*)
Ouch! See – you're always beating me . . . !

KATHARINE
You bastard, I was believing you! You should be
my slave.

*They embrace, he lies over her, considering her naked
back.*

ALMÁSY
I claim this shoulder blade – no, wait – I want –
turn over – I want this!

*He turns her over, kisses her throat, then traces the hollow
indentation.*

ALMÁSY
This place, I love this place, what's it called –
this is mine!
            (KATHARINE *doesn't know*)
I'm going to ask the king permission to call it
the *Almásy Bosphorous.*

KATHARINE
(*teasing*)
I thought we were against ownership?
            (ALMÁSY *acknowledges the irony*)
I can stay tonight.

The luxury of this makes them both sad. The duplicity.
ALMÁSY *rolls away onto his back.*

ALMÁSY
Madox knows, I think. He keeps talking about
Anna Karenina. I think it's his idea of a man-to-
man chat. It's my idea of a man-to-man chat.

KATHARINE
This is a different world – is what I tell myself. A
different life. And here I am a different wife.

ALMÁSY
Yes. Here you are a different wife.

Int. Cab, Cairo street, o/s Shepheard's Hotel. Night

*The cab driver is asleep. In the back of the car GEOFFREY
has opened the champagne. He lets it overflow, then takes
a swig. He fusses with the tissue paper from the bottle,
unravelling it, revealing a chain of hearts.*

Ext. Almásy's house, Old Cairo. Dawn

*ALMÁSY and KATHARINE wander out of his building and
into the early morning streets, hand in hand.*

Ext. Spice market, Cairo. Dawn

*The morning prayers rise out from the city's three
Minarets. They stop at a stall, which is just preparing to
open for the day. KATHARINE examines the collection of
silver thimbles, picks one up.*

KATHARINE
These are darling. What are they, thimbles?

ALMÁSY
Yes. It's full of saffron, just in case you think I'm
giving it to you to encourage your sewing.

He points it out to the merchant who gives him a price.
Without comment, ALMÁSY produces the money and,
beaming, hands the thimble to KATHARINE.

ALMÁSY
I don't care to bargain.

KATHARINE
That day, had you followed me to the market?

ALMÁSY
Yes, of course.

KATHARINE
(*loving him, but frightened*)
Shall we be all right?

ALMÁSY
Yes. Yes.
(*shrugs*)
Absolutely.

Ext. Cairo street. Dawn

KATHARINE *takes leave of ALMÁSY on the street corner*
away from the hotel entrance. They don't kiss. There's a
moment when their hands brush, linger, then she leaves
him at the top of the stairs and disappears.

Int. Cab, Cairo street, o/s Shepheard's Hotel. Day

GEOFFREY, *unshaven, slumped in the taxi, watches as*
KATHARINE *crosses the street and heads toward the hotel.*
His expression is terrible, trying to smile, his face
collapsed.

Int. The Patient's room. Morning

'Cheek to Cheek' leaks into the room from a gramophone that CARAVAGGIO *stands over proudly.* THE PATIENT *opens his eyes – is confused, dislocated – stares blankly at* CARAVAGGIO.

> CARAVAGGIO
> (*grinning*)
> Thought you'd never wake up!

> THE PATIENT
> What?

HANA *comes in, sleepily, frowns at the gramophone.*

> HANA
> Where did you find that?

> CARAVAGGIO
> I liberated it.

> HANA
> I think that's called looting.

> CARAVAGGIO
> (*relaxed*)
> No one should own music. The real question is, who wrote the song?

> THE PATIENT
> Irving Berlin.

> CARAVAGGIO
> For?

> THE PATIENT
> *Top Hat.*

CARAVAGGIO
Is there a song you don't know?

HANA
(speaking for him)
No. He sings all the time.

She goes over to THE PATIENT *and kisses him gently.*

HANA
Good morning.
(of his singing)
Did you know that? You're always singing.

THE PATIENT
I've been told before.

HANA
Kip's another one.

She goes to the window, looks over to where the tents are pitched, sees HARDY *shaving and* KIP *in the process of washing his hair, his turban hanging like a ribbon between two trees to dry. He's perched over a bowl and is dipping his long, coal-black hair into it. As* HANA *watches* KIP, CARAVAGGIO *changes the record.* THE PATIENT *identifies it immediately.*

THE PATIENT
'Wang Wang Blues.'

CARAVAGGIO
You're incredible!

Ext. Monastery garden. Morning

HANA *walks toward the tent, and passes* HARDY. *She's carrying a small cup, which she's a little furtive about.*

97

He's carrying a whole armada of oil lamps. He nods upstairs.

HARDY

Good morning, miss.

HANA

Hello. You saved my life. I haven't forgotten.
(HARDY *waves that away*)
I thought you were very, very tall. You seemed so big and – a giant! – and I felt like a child who can't keep her balance.

HARDY
(*does a little mime*)

A toddler.

HANA
(*smiles*)

A toddler.

She goes on outside, and tentatively approaches KIP, who's still working at his hair.

HANA

My hair was long. At some point. I've forgotten what a nuisance it is to wash.

He continues to wash. She holds up the cup of oil.

HANA

Try this. I found a great jar of it. Olive oil.

KIP

Thank you.

She stands for a second, just wanting to be close, then shyly walks away. KIP examines the oil, calls after her.

KIP

Is this for my hair?

HANA
(*turning, smiling*)
Yes, for your hair.

Int. The Patient's room. Evening

CARAVAGGIO *is with* THE PATIENT. *They sit lost in the jazz they're listening to.* THE PATIENT *regards* CARAVAGGIO.

THE PATIENT
There was a general who wore a patch over a
perfectly good eye. The men fought harder for
him. Sometimes I think I could get up and dance.

CARAVAGGIO *doesn't respond.*

THE PATIENT
What's under your mittens?
(*still nothing from* CARAVAGGIO)
What's under your mittens?

CARAVAGGIO *stands, goes to him, removing his mittens.*

Int. British Headquarters, Tobruk, June 1942. Day

CARAVAGGIO, *thumbs intact and wearing a crumpled linen suit, walks through the mangled corridors of British HQ. Smoke is rising from buildings, the ominous scream of Stuka dive-bombers in the distance as the harbour is pounded, the steady thud of explosions. Tobruk is under siege. BHQ is a place in the throes of dismantling itself. Secretaries are visiting braziers manned by Arab boys who*

*stoke the fires as boxes of restricted papers are fed into
them. Ashes hover in the air.*

Int. BHQ, Tobruk. Day

CARAVAGGIO *walks through a large room crowded with
desks. From one of them, a young woman,* AICHA, *frowning at the chaos and the shelling, approaches him.*
AICHA *is* CARAVAGGIO's *sometime lover.*

> AICHA
> He's waiting for you. I'll see you tonight?

Int. Corridor of British Headquarters, Tobruk. Day

FENELON-BARNES *and* CARAVAGGIO *make their way
down the stairs and to the entrance.* AICHA *passes them
on the stairs, looks anxiously at* CARAVAGGIO.

> FENELON-BARNES
> Look, Moose, we need you to stay in Tobruk. I
> know it's a bit of a short straw but the thinking is
> we'll be back – I mean, *we will, we will* be back –
> but we need eyes and ears on the ground. Jerry's
> got our maps, you know. Swine. Before the war
> we helped them run about the desert making
> maps – and now they're getting spies into Cairo
> using our maps, they'll get Rommel into Cairo
> using our maps. The whole of the desert's like a
> bloody bus route and we gave it to them. Any
> foreigner who turned up – 'Welcome to the
> Royal Geographic, take our maps.' Old Madox
> went mad, you know – did you know Peter
> Madox? Magnificent explorer – after he found
> out he'd been betrayed by Almásy, his best
> friend. Absolutely destroyed the poor sod. I'd
> love to get that bastard Almásy. Settle the score.

Ext. Tobruk. Day

The Germans invade Tobruk. They drop to the ground in cluster of parachutes. The harbour rocks with explosions.

Ext. Tobruk dockside. Day

A German troop carrier rumbles forward passing a line of bedraggled British POWs as they're marched along the side of the harbour; passing a dock in which the mangled carcasses of boats send up plumes of ugly smoke.

Ext. Tobruk Square. Day

A crowd of Tobruk civilians – French and Italians among the mostly Arab faces. Their papers are being thoroughly checked by officers sitting at open desks. In a line, wearing his shabby suit, is CARAVAGGIO. An Arab woman in front of him is arguing over the identity of her ominous Caucasian-looking baby. An interpreter mediates. The officer doesn't believe the woman. She's getting frantic at the possibility of losing her child.

Suddenly there's a disturbance as another woman is dragged along the line by her hair. She's bloodied, and has been tortured, and it's hard to recognize her as the pretty AICHA. She is forced to consider some horrified members of the line, shakes her head, moans, falls to her feet. CARAVAGGIO doesn't look, stares straight ahead. An officer watches him as he turns briefly and helplessly out of concern for her. Their eyes catch for an instant and the officer sees it.

CARAVAGGIO slowly walks away from the line. A soldier shouts to halt, the crowd ducks for cover. CARAVAGGIO puts up his arms in surrender.

Int. Interrogation room, Tobruk. Day

CARAVAGGIO *is slumped at a table, his hands manacled to its thick wooden legs. There's a telephone at another table in the corner of the room attended by a* CLERK *with a* STENOGRAPHER *working next to him. The room has stone walls which appear damp, and no windows. Soldiers stand guard at the door. It's a horrible room.* CARAVAGGIO *is trying to sleep, he's unshaven and pasty-looking. His interrogator,* MULLER, *seems incredibly tired and aggravated. He approaches the table carrying a collection of photographs which he lays down on the table in front of* CARAVAGGIO.

> MULLER

David Caravaggio.

> CARAVAGGIO

No.

> MULLER
> (*of the photographs*)

This was taken in Cairo at British Headquarters
– July '41. And so was this – August '41. And
this – February '42.

> CARAVAGGIO

It's possible. I was buying or selling something.
I've been to Cairo many times.

> MULLER

You are a Canadian spy working for the Allies.
Code name Moose.

The phone rings again, is answered. The CLERK *calls to* MULLER, *who gets up, irritably.* CARAVAGGIO *addresses the room.*

CARAVAGGIO
Could you get me a doctor? I'm sick, I'm leaking
blood.

Nobody responds. MULLER *is irascible on the phone,
checking his watch, negotiating time. The call finishes.*

CLERK
(*in German*)
He's asking for a doctor.

MULLER
(*to* CARAVAGGIO)
You want a doctor?

CARAVAGGIO
I've been asking for weeks, months, I don't
know –

MULLER
We don't have a doctor, but we do have a nurse.

CARAVAGGIO
(*taken aback*)
A nurse? Well, sure, great. A nurse would be
great. A nurse? Great.

MULLER *nods at the* CLERK, *who instantly gets up. Just
then the telephone rings again. He hesitates.*

MULLER
(*in German*)
Leave it and get the nurse!

The CLERK *exits.*

MULLER
(*turns to* CARAVAGGIO)
Look – give me something. A name. A code. So
we can all get out of this room.
(*wiping his face*)
I'm sick of this heat. It's too hot.

CARAVAGGIO
I slept with a girl. I've got a wife in Tripoli. A
girl comes up and points at you, you only see
trouble.

The NURSE *comes in. She is Arab, unbearably young,
pure. Her head is covered.*

MULLER
I'll tell you what I'm going to do. This is your
nurse, by the way. She's Moslem, so she'll
understand all of this. What's the punishment
for adultery? Let's leave it at that. You're
married and you were fucking another woman,
so that's – is it the hands that are cut off? Or is
that for stealing? Does anyone know?

There's a silence. MULLER *turns to* CARAVAGGIO.

MULLER
Well, you must know. You were brought up in
Libya, yes?

CARAVAGGIO
Don't cut me.

MULLER
Or was it Toronto?

Now the phone starts again. The CLERK *picks it up,*

there's a terse exchange, he puts the receiver on the desk, waits for the moment to interrupt MULLER.

MULLER

Ten fingers. How about this? You give me a name for every finger – doesn't matter who. I get something, you keep something. I'm trying to be reasonable.

CARAVAGGIO
(*ashen*)

Don't cut me. Come on.

MULLER
(*pauses, suddenly puzzled*)

Are thumbs fingers?
(*in German to the others*)
Is a thumb a finger?

No response. MULLER *opens his palms to* CARAVAGGIO.

MULLER

I get no help from these people.

MULLER *slams down the telephone receiver. An air raid siren is going off somewhere, and now the faint sound of explosions is also discernible, but all muffled in this room along with the steady tap-tap of the* STENOGRAPHER. *At that moment,* MULLER *suddenly becomes aware of what is happening. He turns on the* STENOGRAPHER.

MULLER
(*in German*)

What are you doing?

STENOGRAPHER
(*awkward, in German*)

The Geneva Convention, I'm –

MULLER *peremptorily rips out the paper, throws it on the floor.*

MULLER
The Geneva Convention! Ach!

CARAVAGGIO
Hey – Come on! You can't do that!

During this MULLER's *gone to the table, pulled out a drawer, and produced a cutthroat razor. He hands it to the* NURSE, *makes a line across his own left thumb, and jerks his head toward* CARAVAGGIO. *The* NURSE *is extremely reluctant.* MULLER *claps his hands, pushes her towards* CARAVAGGIO.

MULLER
Go! Hey! Go!

CARAVAGGIO *is in terror.*

CARAVAGGIO
I'll give you names. I'll give you names. What names did you say? I've forgotten the names. Tell me the names and I'll agree.

The guards come away from the door and press down on CARAVAGGIO's *shoulders to prevent him from moving. The* NURSE, *grim-faced, approaches, kneels at the table, takes the blade from* MULLER, *takes gentle hold of* CARAVAGGIO's *hand.*

CARAVAGGIO
(*as she prepares to cut*)
Please – please – oh, please – oh, please – I promise. What name did you say? I knew them!

107

(*jabbing at the* NURSE)

Come on!

And then CARAVAGGIO *screams and screams. The air raid is continuing outside, the phone is ringing.* MULLER *watches as* CARAVAGGIO *is mutilated, his cries continuing, his whimpers horrible.*

Int. The Patient's room. Night

CARAVAGGIO, *his hands revealed, thumbless, advances on* THE PATIENT, *his cries still ringing in the room.*

CARAVAGGIO
The man who took my thumbs, I found him
eventually – I killed him. The man who took my
photograph, I found him too – that took me a
year. He's dead. Another man helped get that
man across the desert to Cairo. I've been looking
for him.

Int. Library of the Department of Egyptology, Cairo, 1939. Day

MADOX *and* ALMÁSY *are camped in one corner of the library, hunched over their maps and papers and journals and clashing furiously over the site of the next part of the expedition.*

MADOX
(*pushing away his charts*)
You can't get through there.

ALMÁSY
I was looking again at Bell's maps. If we can find

a way to cross the wadi we can drive straight up
into Cairo . . .
> (*he points at a map*)
– and this whole spur is a real possibility . . .

MADOX

So, on Thursday you don't trust Bell's map –
'Bell was a fool, Bell couldn't draw a map' – but
on Friday he's suddenly infallible?

ALMÁSY *is surprised by* MADOX'*s anger.*

MADOX

And where are the Expedition Maps?

ALMÁSY

In my room.

MADOX

Those maps belong to His Majesty's
Government. They shouldn't be left lying
around for any Tom, Dick, or Harry to have
sight of.

ALMÁSY

What on earth's the matter with you?

MADOX

Don't be so bloody naive. You know there's a
war breaking out.
> (*he tosses a slip of paper onto the map,*
> *recites its message*)
This arrived this morning. By order of the
British Government – all International
Expeditions to be aborted by May 1939.

Ext. Cairo souk. Late afternoon

ALMÁSY *and* MADOX *walk through the souk, the bars filling up as the stalls are closing. Both of them are sombre.*

ALMÁSY
What do they care about our maps?

MADOX
What do we find in the desert? Arrowheads, spears. In a war, if you own the desert, you own North Africa.

ALMÁSY
(*contemptuous*)
Own the desert.

ALMÁSY *hesitates at a junction, clearly about to take his leave of* MADOX.

ALMÁSY
Madox – that place, that place at the base of a woman's throat? You know, the hollow, *here* – does it have an official name?

MADOX *looks at him.*

MADOX
For God's sake, man – pull yourself together.

Int. Open-air cinema, Cairo. Evening

The open-air cinema is just beginning its evening programme.

Pathé News begins and we date the event to April 1939. Stories of imminent war jostle with images of Merrie England. Village greens, sporting victories, record sun-

shine on the Isle of Wight. Alone among the necking couples — mostly soldiers with their Egyptian girlfriends — sits KATHARINE. *She's waiting for* ALMÁSY. KATHARINE *is wretched. She sits, head down, hardly watching the screen, marooned in her despair about duplicity, sordid assignations.*

ALMÁSY *arrives, slides in beside* KATHARINE, *his shadow momentarily large across the screen.*

ALMÁSY

Sorry.

They watch the screen. KATHARINE *is weeping.* ALMÁSY *doesn't understand. He puts his arm around her.*

KATHARINE

I can't do this, I can't do this anymore.

Int. Open-air cinema, Cairo. Evening

Later and KATHARINE *and* ALMÁSY *sit stiffly under the bleachers while the main feature — a Busby Berkeley revue — plays in the background. Finally,* KATHARINE *gets up.*

KATHARINE

I'd better go now. Say goodbye here.

ALMÁSY

I'm not agreeing. Don't think I'm agreeing, because I'm not.

They stand, awkward. KATHARINE *rehearses her position.*

KATHARINE

Any minute now, he'll find out, we'll barge into
someone – it will kill him.

ALMÁSY

Don't go over it again, please.

*He takes her hands, lays his cheeks into them. She pulls
her hands away as she makes for the exit. He calls after
her.*

ALMÁSY

Katharine –

He looks toward her, his smile awful.

ALMÁSY

I just wanted you to know. I'm not missing you
yet.

She nods, can't find this funny.

KATHARINE

You will. You will.

*She turns sharply from him and bangs her head against the
bleacher support, staggers at the shock of it, then hurries
away.*

Int. The Patient's room. Night

THE PATIENT's *stertorous breathing, each intake accompanied by a small noise, a note, suddenly stops. Then it
steadies again. He appears to be alone.* CARAVAGGIO *lies
under his bed, smoking, a vigil.*

Int. Ambassador's residence, Cairo, 1939. Night

Last seen at the troops' Christmas party, the inner courtyard has been transformed into an elegant outdoor banquet, with a small band providing entertainment. The ALMÁSY/MADOX *team is assembled for a farewell dinner. They are waiting for* ALMÁSY *to arrive, his seat conspicuously empty. He is very late. And then he's there, dangerously drunk, terribly dashing. He practically dances to his chair, which he drags violently away from its position opposite* KATHARINE. *He bows to* LADY HAMPTON.

ALMÁSY
I believe I'm rather late.

MADOX
(*ignoring the drama of this entrance*)
Good, we're all here? A toast, to the
International Sand Club – may it soon resurface.

THE OTHERS
The International Sand Club!

ALMÁSY
(*raising his glass*)
The International Sand Club! Misfits, buggers,
fascists, and fools. God bless us, everyone.

The others drink, trying to ignore his mood.

ALMÁSY
Oops! Mustn't say *International*. Dirty word.
Filthy word. His Majesty! *Die Führer! Il Duce!*

CLIFTON
Sorry, what's your point?

ALMÁSY
(*not responding*)
And the people here don't want us. You must be
joking. The Egyptians are desperate to get rid of
the Colonials . . .
(*to an embarrassed* FOUAD)
Isn't that right, Fouad? Some of their best people
down on their hands and knees begging to be
spared a knighthood . . .
(*to his host,* SIR HAMPTON)
Isn't that right? Isn't that right, Sir Ronnie?

RONNIE HAMPTON *shrugs. They're all very uncomfortable.* ALMÁSY *turns to* CLIFTON.

ALMÁSY
What's my point?
(*standing up*)
Oh! I've invented a new dance – anybody up for
it – it's called – it's called – the Bosphorus Hug.
Madox? Bermann? You'll dance with me . . .
D'Ag? Come on D'Aggers.

D'AGOSTINO
Let's eat first. Sit down.

The band is now playing 'Manhattan'. ALMÁSY, *without
missing a beat, begins to sing, replacing the words with
alternatives he knows. He lurches around.* KATHARINE
can't look at him.

ALMÁSY
'. . . We'll bathe at Brighton, the fish you'll
frighten when you're in – your bathing suit so
thin, will make the shellfish grin, fin to fin.'
They're playing it far too slowly, but these were

the words, actually, before they were cleaned up.
Might be a song for you, Mrs Clif –

MADOX *gets up and pulls* ALMÁSY *into his chair, taking charge.*

> MADOX
> (*whispering sharply*)
> Look, either shut up, or go home. You're
> completely plastered! Now sit down.

> ALMÁSY
> (*loudly*)
> Absolutely right, shut up, shut up. Sorry. I'm so
> sorry. I can't think what came over me. *Lashings*
> of apologies – all around.

Ext. Ambassador's residence. Night

Later, and now most of the group are dancing. We see
KATHARINE *dancing with* RUPERT DOUGLAS, *enjoying*
herself. BERMANN *is there and even* MADOX – *jogging and*
grinning foolishly. CLIFTON *looks at* KATHARINE, *who,*
as the dance ends, excuses herself to go to the cloakroom.
ALMÁSY *hovers in the shadows, unseen.*

Int. Ambassador's residence. Night

KATHARINE *comes along the familiar warren of rooms*
and corridors and is suddenly confronted by ALMÁSY,
tortured and out of control.

> ALMÁSY
> Why were you holding his collar?

> KATHARINE
> What?

ALMÁSY
(*mimicking her inflection*)
What? That boy, that little boy, you were
holding his collar, you were gripping his collar,
what for? Is he next? You going to drag him into
your little room? Where is it? Is this it?

KATHARINE
Don't do this.

ALMÁSY
(*pressing her against the wall*)
I've watched you – I've watched you at garden
parties, on verandahs, at the races – how can
you stand there? How can you *ever* smile? As if
your life hadn't capsized?

KATHARINE
You know why. You know why.

He tries to hold her. She resists. They're both in torment.

ALMÁSY
Dance with me.

KATHARINE
No.

ALMÁSY
(*tracing her shoulder blade*)
Dance with me. I want to touch you. I want the
things which are mine. Which belong to me.

KATHARINE
(*sobbing*)
Do you think you're the only one who feels
anything? Is that what you think?

Int. The Patient's room. Night

HANA *sits with* THE PATIENT. *His eyes are full of tears. He opens them, sees her watching over him. He's embarrassed.*

THE PATIENT
Why don't you go? Get some sleep.

HANA
Would you like me to?

He nods. She gets up from her sewing, then leaves.

Int. The monastery, landing and stairs. Night

HANA *leaves the room, then turns and sees a tiny lamp on the floor. It's made from a snail shell filled with oil. She bends to it curiously, then sees a second lamp half-way down the stairs, then a third further down. She smiles in the light, then follows the trail.*

Ext. The monastery cloisters. Night

In the cloisters the trail of shell lamps continues, like tiny cat's eyes. As they reach the hopscotch chalk marks, they outline the squares. HANA *hopscotches and then follows the lights, disappearing around a corner.*

Int. The monastery stables. Night

HANA *comes through into the stables. The lamps lead her, then they stop. She peers into the shadows.*

KIP (o/s)
Hana.

She turns to the voice. He steps out of the darkness.

HANA
(happy)

Kip.

And he goes to her.

Ext. Arezzo. Dusk

Kip, Hana clinging onto him, steers the motorbike in the deserted piazza. They dismount and walk up to the doors of the church.

Int. Church. Dusk

They enter the church. It's in almost total darkness. Kip circles Hana with the rope, making a sling across her waist and shoulder. He lights a small flare and hands it to her before disappearing into the gloom.

Hana stands holding the flare.

Kip runs up a hill of sandbags, right up into the rafters. He collects the other end of the rope that is attached to Hana. Holding on to it, he just steps off into the darkness.

Simultaneously Hana is swung up into the air, her startled yelp echoing around the church. Kip touches ground, while Hana swings through space, coming to rest about three feet from the frescoed walls, painted by Piero della Francesca. Hana's flare makes a halo around her head.

Now Kip, on the ground, still holding the rope, walks forward and causes Hana to swing to the right. She lets out a giddy laugh, exhilarated and nervous, and she flies, illuminating – en passant – faces, bodies, angels. Kip

guides the rope as if they were making love, which in a way they are.

HANA arrives, hovering, in front of the Queen of Sheba talking to Solomon. She's overwhelmed. She reaches out to touch the giant neck of the sad Queen.

Int. Kip's tent. Night

HANA lies over KIP in the stable, a naked white body plaited into a brown one.

HANA

If one night I didn't come to see you, what
would you do?

KIP

I try not to expect you.

HANA

Yes, but if it got late and I hadn't shown up?

KIP

Then I'd think there must be a reason.

HANA

You wouldn't come to find me?
(KIP *shrugs*)
That makes me never want to come here.
(KIP *still won't respond*)
Then I tell myself he spends all day searching, in
the night he wants to be found.

Then KIP turns, rolling over to face her.

KIP

I do. I do want you to find me. I do want to be
found. I do.

Ext. The monastery stables. Early morning

HARDY *knocks cautiously on the door of the stables.*
Eventually HANA *opens the door.*

HARDY

Ah, I was looking for Lieutenant Singh.

HANA

He's sleeping.

HARDY

Only we've got to go to work.

HANA

I'll tell him. What is it? Is it a mine?

HARDY

It's a bomb. Up by the viaduct.

She closes the door, then reappears.

HANA

Does he have to go?

HARDY

Pardon me?

HANA

What if you couldn't find him . . . ?
              (HARDY's *bewildered*)
Sergeant, not today, please. Not this morning.

KIP *comes to the door, winding his turban.*

KIP

What's happening? Am I needed?

HARDY

I'm afraid so, sir.

KIP *hurries to his tent.* HANA *follows him.*

HANA

Don't go. I'm frightened.

KIP

This is what I do. I do this every day.

Ext. A viaduct north of the monastery. Day

KIP *is lowered by a pulley into the shaft the sappers have made around the bomb.* HARDY *supervises. The bomb's huge – 2,000 pounds – and protrudes ostrich-like from the pit, its nose sunk into a pool of sludge at the base of the viaduct.*

KIP *steps off and sinks knee-deep in mud, grunting in disgust. Warily, he touches his huge opponent, feeling the condition of the case. He wipes the metal. Reveals a serial number, calls it out to* HARDY, *who's perched on the bank.*

KIP

Serial number – KK–1P2600

KIP *stares at the number. A bomb with his name on it.*

HARDY
(*noting it down*)

KK–1P2600 sir! I'll get the oxygen.

Ext. Road approaching viaduct. Day

HANA *cycles along on* CARAVAGGIO's *bicycle. A tank comes roaring up behind her, then a second and third, loaded up with people – citizens and soldiers, and children – waving flags and gesticulating. She lets the metal circus go by.*

Int. Bomb shaft. Day

Back in the shaft, KIP *works away, his fingers shaking with the cold from the oxygen he's using to freeze the fuse. Suddenly there's a violent tremor. The ground is shuddering, and* KIP's *tools are falling into the sludge.*

KIP
Hardy! What's happening?!

Ext. Viaduct. Day

The tanks are rumbling toward the viaduct. Horns start sounding. HARDY, *below, bellows at his men above for explanation.*

HARDY
Corporal!?

DADE
(*leaning over the parapet of the viaduct*)
Tanks, sir. Don't know what it's about.

HARDY
(*incredulous*)
Stop them!

KIP
Hardy!

HARDY
What is this – a bloody carnival? Stop them!

KIP
The fuse has snapped!

Two sappers run across the bridge toward the oncoming procession. They wave their orange flags, the tanks wave back with their flags – Stars and Stripes, Union Jacks. Now shots are ringing out. In the shaft, oblivious, KIP slides out from under the bomb, the oxygen spurting everywhere, all over his clothes, hissing on the surface of the water. HARDY bends into the shaft, heedless of his own safety.

HARDY
You've got to cut, sir, that frost won't last.

KIP
Go away.

HARDY
Yessir.

KIP
This is making me incredibly angry.

HARDY
I know, sir.

KIP rubs his hands to warm them up, locates his needle pliers, and slips them through the tiny gap. His hand touches the casing and the freeze burns his hand. He jerks back, dropping the pliers into the watery sludge, cursing.

Above them the tanks are rumbling over the bridge, sending drizzles of dust onto them from the fragile structure. The cheering continues, oblivious to the crisis below.

Now Kip's on his hands and knees in the sludge, trying frantically to find the pliers. Hardy looks at his watch, he can't help. The seconds run out as Kip grovels in the mud.

HARDY

Can you feel them?

Then, suddenly Kip emerges with the pliers, soaked, shuddering. He doesn't know where to cut.

HARDY

Cut it, sir, you've got to cut it!

He goes straight to an exposed loop, no finesse, and cuts. There's a snip. Then nothing.

Ext. Viaduct. Day

Kip and Hardy emerge from their ordeal to join what appears to be a party. There are wine bottles and embraces. They're bewildered.

HARDY

Get a blanket!
                    (*not getting attention*)
Spalding – get a blanket for the Lieutenant!

DADE

It's over, sir! It's over. Jerry's surrendered.
                    (*to Kip*)
Well done, well done, sir!

And now they're all shaking hands and slapping backs, and the soldiers from the tanks are there and the victory celebrations begin. KIP's blank, drained, not taking anything in, as DADE wraps a blanket around his shoulders.

HANA arrives on the bicycle and she and KIP embrace privately amidst the celebrations. A different kind of victory for them.

Int. The Patient's room. Night

Thunder breaks over the monastery. HANA suddenly comes to the door of the room. She looks mischievous.

> HANA
>
> It's raining.

And then she bursts out laughing.

Ext. The monastery cloisters. Morning

A whoop precedes the headlong rush of KIP, HARDY, and CARAVAGGIO as they cart THE PATIENT across the cloisters like manic stretcher-bearers. HANA is with them, checking on THE PATIENT, who bounces uncomfortably. He is nervous, a little giddy, but laughing. He tries to say something.

> CARAVAGGIO
>
> What's he saying?

> HANA
>
> He's saying it's wonderful.

The rain buckets down as they circle the pond, HANA's umbrella threatening to lift her into the air.

Int. The Patient's room. Night

A victory celebration party.

The gramophone plays. KIP sits in the window, the shutter open, the village lit up behind his head, nodding to the music, sucking out of his condensed milk. Elsewhere there is an open bottle of cognac, some wine. THE PATIENT has a beaker of wine. CARAVAGGIO is dancing with HANA.

> HANA

Kip – come and dance with us.

> KIP
> *(a sly wobble of the head)*

Later.

> HANA

Oh, come on.

THE PATIENT watches, his head nodding to the music.

> THE PATIENT

Yeah!

Ext. Village square. Night

A tiny piazza where the sappers and the villagers are having their own, more raucous, Victory Feste. There are accordions, there's dancing, and there's HARDY, stripped to some exotic underpants, clambering up the statue of a First-World-War soldier in the middle of the fountain. It's currently sporting a German helmet and HARDY has a British replacement in his hands. He also has a Union Jack flag between his teeth. He's extremely drunk and extremely happy.

The rest of the Bomb Squad and the other partygoers roar their approval.

Int. The Patient's room. Night

HANA and CARAVAGGIO are still dancing.

There's a muffled thud in the distance. KIP's ears prick up. He glances for an instant out of the window.

> HANA
> (anxious, of the noise)
> What was that?

She is spinning with CARAVAGGIO. When she comes around again, KIP has gone.

Ext. Village square, Italy 1945. Night

KIP's motorbike skids into the tiny piazza.

A military ambulance is already there. The shattered fountain, the sluiced flagstones, shining wet and slick, give some clues as to what's happened, as do the elderly standing in the shadows, the distressed girls, arm in arm. One girl, young and quite striking, is particularly inconsolable, her grief sobbed out at the doors of the ambulance.

SPALDING salutes KIP, who waves his salute away, just wanting to know what happened.

> SPALDING
> Booby trap. Sergeant Hardy was running up the Union Jack, sir, up off that statue – it just went off, sir.

DADE

Sergeant Hardy climbed up, sir, just for a lark.
Should have been me, it was my idea.

KIP *goes to the ambulance.* SPALDING *tries to stop him.*

SPALDING

Sir – you don't want to look.

KIP *steps into the back of the ambulance, bends over both
bodies, does look, then comes out, past the weeping girl.*

KIP

Who's that girl?

DADE

His fiancée, sir.

KIP
(*confused*)

Hardy's?

DADE

He kept it a bit dark.

Ext. The stables. Late day

HANA *approaches.* KIP *is inside the stable, the door
latched. He sits, impassively, still shocked, as* HANA *tries
to make contact.*

HANA

Kip. Kip. It's me. I'm so sorry about what happened.
(*no response*)
Can I talk to you?
(*no response*)
Why won't you talk to me? I don't understand.
Let me come in.

She kicks at the door in her frustration. KIP doesn't move, doesn't appear to hear.

HANA

Please, Kip, please!

KIP doesn't respond. HANA is at a loss.

Int. Patient's room. Evening

THE PATIENT *listens as* HANA *comes back into the monastery, climbs the stone steps to her room. He doesn't know what's happening. Feels desperately isolated.*

THE PATIENT

Hana? Hana?

Int. Hana's room. Evening

Later, and HANA *sits in her room, despondent, lost in her thoughts. Then she is distracted by conversation in* THE PATIENT's *room below.*

Int. The Patient's room. Night

THE PATIENT's *eyes open to see* CARAVAGGIO *at the morphine.*

THE PATIENT

Hana tells me you're leaving.

CARAVAGGIO
(preparing the injection)

There's going to be trials, they want me to interpret, don't they know I'm allergic to courtrooms?

He delivers the injection into THE PATIENT's *arm.* THE
PATIENT *sighs.* CARAVAGGIO *takes off his jacket. A pistol
is stuck in his waistband, and he places it ominously on the
altar.* THE PATIENT *sees it.*

> CARAVAGGIO

So, I come across the Hospital Convoy –
> (*holds up the syringe*)

– I'm looking for this stuff, and this nurse, Mary,
tells me about you and Hana, hiding in some
monastery, in – retreat –
> (*he administers his own injection,*
> *using his teeth to grip the sleeve*)

– how you came out of the desert and you
were burned and you didn't remember your
name but you knew the words to every song
that ever was and you had one possession – a
copy of *Herodotus* – and it was filled with
letters and cuttings and then I knew it was
you.
> (*he glares at* THE PATIENT)

I saw you writing in that book. At the Embassy
in Cairo, when I had thumbs and you had a face
and a name.

> THE PATIENT

I see.

Upstairs, sitting on her bed, HANA *listens with increasing
concern.*

> CARAVAGGIO

Before you went over to the Germans, before
you got Rommel's spy across the desert and
inside British Headquarters. He took some
pretty good photographs – I saw mine in that

torture room in Tobruk, so – they made an impression.

THE PATIENT
I had to get back to the desert. I made a promise. The rest meant nothing to me.

CARAVAGGIO
What did you say?

THE PATIENT
The rest meant nothing to me.

CARAVAGGIO
There was a result to what you did. It wasn't just another *expedition.*

(*holds up hands*)

It did this. If the British hadn't unearthed that photographer, thousands of people could have died.

THE PATIENT
Thousands of people did die, just different people.

CARAVAGGIO
Yes, like Madox?

THE PATIENT
What?!

CARAVAGGIO
You know he shot himself – your best friend? When he found out you were a spy.

THE PATIENT
(*appalled*)
No. Madox thought I was a spy? No. No. I was
never a spy.

Ext. Base camp at the Cave of Swimmers, 1939. Day

*The expedition team is packing up the Base Camp.
Madox and Almásy are walking together toward the
plateau where Fouad, Al Auf, and others work at the
cars.*

MADOX
It's ghastly, it's like a witch hunt – anybody
remotely foreign is suddenly a spy, so watch out.

ALMÁSY
Right.

MADOX
We didn't care about countries. Did we? Brits,
Arabs, Hungarians, Germans. None of that
mattered, did it? It was something finer than
that.

ALMÁSY
Yes. It was.

MADOX
When's Clifton picking you up?

ALMÁSY
Tomorrow afternoon. Don't worry, I'll be ready.

MADOX
I'll leave the plane in Kufra Oasis. So if you need

it . . . hard to know how long one's talking about. We might all be back in a month or two.

Madox kneels and takes a handful of sand, puts it into his pocket. Almásy puts out a hand. This is a moment of great emotional weight for them both, conducted as if nothing were happening.

MADOX

I have to teach myself not to read too much into everything. Comes of too long having to read so much into hardly anything at all.

ALMÁSY

Goodbye, my friend.

They shake hands.

MADOX
(in Arabic)
May God make safety your companion.

ALMÁSY
(a tradition)
There is no God.
(smiles)
But I hope someone looks after you.

Madox clambers up the hill, then remembers something, jabs at his throat.

MADOX

In case you're still wondering – this is called the suprasternal notch.

Almásy nods.

MADOX

Come and visit us in Dorset. When all this
nonsense is over.
            (*then shrugs, thick with feeling*)
You'll never come to Dorset.

ALMÁSY *watches* MADOX *leave.*

Int. Patient's room. Day

THE PATIENT *is still digesting the news of* MADOX's
suicide. CARAVAGGIO *is a little surprised at his response.*

CARAVAGGIO

You didn't know Madox killed himself? And you
didn't kill the Cliftons?

THE PATIENT

No. No.
            (*now he is overwhelmed by the pain
                of his memory*)
She . . . she . . .
            (*then suddenly he's clear*)
Well, maybe I did. Maybe I did.

Unseen to either of them HANA *listens, full of emotion, as
the story unfolds.*

Ext. Base Camp at the Cave of Swimmers, 1939. Day

ALMÁSY *sits on a ridge transferring map information from
his Herodotus onto a sheet of paper. He looks up at the
sound of* CLIFTON's *approaching Steerman. It passes fast
and horribly close to his head.*

THE PATIENT (o/s)

I was packing up the Base Camp at the Cave of

Swimmers. Clifton had arranged to fly down
from Cairo to collect me. He flew like a
madman, so I didn't take much notice . . .

CLIFTON is flying toward the landing strip. From the air
it's possible to make out ALMÁSY scrambling down from
the ridge toward where stones indicate a landing area,
carrying the last of the materials from the Cave of
Swimmers.

Ext. Base Camp at the Cave of Swimmers. Day

ALMÁSY watches as the plane drops toward him, shielding
his eyes against the sun. He stoops to gather up his
luggage.

ALMÁSY looks up to see the plane swerve, now suddenly
heading straight toward him. He's completely vulnerable,
nowhere to run. He dives at the ground. The plane
smashes against an invisible ridge and turns over and over,
the wings snapping off like twigs as it hurtles past the
prostrate ALMÁSY. He gets to his feet and starts to run
toward the wreckage.

A blue line of smoke is uncoiling from the plane, but no
fire. ALMÁSY pulls away the debris to find GEOFFREY –
slumped, neck broken, bloody. He tries to move him, and
in the process reveals, to his absolute horror, KATHARINE,
staring grimly ahead, unable to move. He's frantic.

ALMÁSY
Katharine! Oh dear God, Katharine – what are
you doing here?

KATHARINE
(eyes rolling, an incredible weariness)
I can't get out. I can't move.

ALMÁSY *starts to pull at the wreck around her. During this —*

KATHARINE
'A surprise,' he said.
          (*she can hardly talk*)
Poor Geoffrey. He knew. He must have known
all the time. He was shouting, 'I love you,
Katharine, I love you so much.' Is he badly hurt?

ALMÁSY
I have to get you out.

ALMÁSY *puts his arms around* KATHARINE *to try and pull her clear. She can't stand the pain.*

KATHARINE
Please don't move me.

ALMÁSY
I have to get you out.

KATHARINE
It hurts too much.

ALMÁSY
          (*can't bear to hurt her*)
I know, my darling, I'm sorry.

He pulls — hard — the pain from which causes KATHARINE *to gasp, then pass out. He lifts her gently into his arms and carries her from the danger of the place.*

Ext. The Cave of Swimmers. Day

ALMÁSY *has wrapped* KATHARINE *in the silk folds of her parachute and emerges from near the familiar cleft in the*

rock, *struggling with the exertion of the climb as they approach the Cave of Swimmers. He has a large water bottle slung around his neck and a haversack, and is loaded like a pack horse.* KATHARINE *opens her eyes.*

KATHARINE
(*whispering*)
Why did you hate me?

ALMÁSY
What?

KATHARINE
Don't you know you drove everybody mad?

ALMÁSY
Shhhh. Don't talk.

KATHARINE
(*gasping*)
You speak so many bloody languages and you
never want to talk.

They stagger on. He suddenly notices a stain of gold at her neck. It's saffron, leaking from a silver thimble which hangs from a black ribbon.

ALMÁSY
(*overwhelmed*)
You're wearing the thimble.

KATHARINE
Of course. You idiot. I always wear it. I've always
worn it. I've always loved you.

ALMÁSY *cries as he walks – huge sobs, no words – convulsed with the pain of it. They approach the Cave.*

Int. Cave of Swimmers. Day

ALMÁSY *comes through in shadows, carrying* KATHAR-
INE, *blocking out the light that pours into the entrance of
the cave. Once inside, he sets her down incredibly gently,
makes a bed of blankets and the parachute. He turns on
his flashlight.*

KATHARINE

It's so cold.

ALMÁSY

I know. I'm sorry. I'll make a fire.

Int. Cave of Swimmers. Torchlight

*As he makes the fire, the light sends his shadow flitting
across the walls.*

KATHARINE

Did you get Geoffrey from the plane?

ALMÁSY
(reluctant)

Yes.

KATHARINE

Thank you.

ALMÁSY
(as he works)

Listen to me, Katharine. You've broken your
ankle and I'm going to have to try and bind it. I
think you've also broken your wrist – and maybe
some ribs, which is why it's hurting you to
breathe. I'm going to have to walk to El Taj.
Although, given the traffic in the desert these
days I'm bound to bump into one army or
another. And then I'll be back and you'll be fine.

The fire is lit and he comes over to her, kneels beside her.

KATHARINE

Do you promise? I wouldn't want to die here. I
don't want to die in the desert. I've always had
rather an elaborate funeral in mind, with
particular hymns. Very English. And I know
exactly where I want to be buried. In our garden.
Where I grew up. With a view of the sea. So
promise me you'll come back for me.

ALMÁSY

I promise I'll come back. I promise I'll never
leave you. Now, you have plenty of water and
food.

He kisses her tenderly. Pulls out his Herodotus and lays it beside her. Then he puts down the flashlight.

ALMÁSY

And a good read.
   (of the flashlight battery)
Don't waste this.

KATHARINE

Thank you.
   (clouds over)
Will you bury Geoffrey? I know he's dead.

ALMÁSY

I'm sorry, Katharine.

KATHARINE

I know.

He's tearing strips from the parachute with his knife.

ALMÁSY

Every night I cut out my heart but in the
morning it was full again.

He leans over her, desperately worried for her. She smiles.

KATHARINE

Darling. My darling.

Ext. The desert. Dawn

ALMÁSY walking. He's singing to keep awake. 'Darktown Strutter's Ball' – 'I'll be down to get you in the taxi, honey . . .'

145

Ext. The desert. Night

ALMÁSY *trudges on.*

> THE PATIENT (o/s)
> I stopped at noon and at twilight. 'Three days
> there,' I told her, 'then three hours back by car.
> Don't go anywhere. I'll be back. I'll be back.'

Ext. The desert. Dusk

ALMÁSY *continues, his journey taking him through miles
of undulating dunes.*

Ext. El Taj. Day

Finally ALMÁSY *arrives at the outskirts of El Taj. He
staggers toward this ancient trading post. A British sentry
watches his approach with interest.*

Ext. Square at El Taj. Day

The sentry, a CORPORAL, *brings* ALMÁSY *into a square.
A young* OFFICER *sits at a table in the shadows of his
office. His staff car is parked in the shade.*

> OFFICER
> Good morning!
> (*the* CORPORAL *has a water bottle, hands it to*
> ALMÁSY)
> So, golly, where have you come from?

> ALMÁSY
> (*gulping the water,
> trying to summon his thoughts*)
> There's been an accident. I need a doctor – to
> come with me. And I need to borrow this car.

I'll pay, of course, and I need, I need morphine
and –

OFFICER
May I see your papers, sir?

ALMÁSY
What?

OFFICER
If I could just see some form of identification?

ALMÁSY
(brain racing)
I'm sorry, I'm not making sense, forgive me, I've
been walking, I've – there's a woman badly
injured at Gilf Kebir, in the Cave of Swimmers.
I am a member of the Royal Geographical
Society.

OFFICER
Right. Now, if I could just take your name.

ALMÁSY
(trying to control his feelings)
Count Laszlo de Almásy.

The OFFICER is writing this down. A glance at his
CORPORAL.

OFFICER
Almásy – would you mind spelling that? What
nationality would that be?

ALMÁSY
Look, listen to me. A woman is dying – my wife!
– is dying. I have been walking for three days! I

do not want to spell my name, I want you to give
me this car!

> OFFICER
> (*writing*)
> I understand you are agitated – perhaps if you'd
> like to sit down I could radio back to HQ – ?

> ALMÁSY
> (*snapping*)
> No! NO! Don't radio anybody, just, just give me
> the fucking car!

ALMÁSY *sets on the* OFFICER, *hauling him by the lapels,
but then immediately loses his balance. As he stumbles up
he gets the stock of the* CORPORAL's *rifle across his head,
knocking him to the ground.*

Int. Cave of Swimmers. Torchlight

KATHARINE *has been writing in the* Herodotus. *The
torchlight flickers as it illuminates some words – 'Drag
myself outside' is legible, then 'We die, we die.' She
shakes the torch. It flickers again. Then goes out. Absolute
blackness. The sound of her trembling breath, of her terror.*

Ext. El Taj street. Day

ALMÁSY, *head pounding, is in the back of the jeep, chained
to the tailgate. He's desperate. The* CORPORAL *is driving.*

> ALMÁSY
> (*shouting, hoarse*)
> Stop the car. Please. A woman is dying!

> CORPORAL
> Listen, Fritz, if I have to listen to another word

from you I'm going to give you a fucking good
hiding.

> ALMÁSY
> Fritz? What are you talking about? Fritz?

> CORPORAL
> That's your name innit? Count Fucking
> Arsehole Von Bismarck? What's that supposed
> to be then, Irish?

ALMÁSY, *beserk, starts to yank at his chains, screaming.*

> ALMÁSY
> Please! You have to listen! Please, listen to me –
> Katharine! Katharine!

Ext. A train, the desert. Dusk

A train scuttles through the desert.

Int. Train, the desert. Dusk

*ALMÁSY is handcuffed to the metal grille of the goods
compartment. He's lying down among a bunch of other
prisoners and their little bundles of possessions in this
makeshift cell – some Arabs, some Italians.*

*A SERGEANT pushes a lavatory-bound prisoner along the
corridor, leaving behind a young PRIVATE who sits on a
packing case, with a rifle across his lap, reading a Penguin
edition of* Gulliver's Travels. *ALMÁSY is in complete
despair to be on the train. He tries to move, but he's locked
tight to the grille. He rattles the cuffs against the metal.*

ALMÁSY

Excuse me.
                    (*the* SOLDIER *looks up*)
I also need to use the lavatory.

SOLDIER

You'll have to wait.

ALMÁSY

It's urgent.

SOLDIER
                    (*calls up the corridor*)
Sarge! Jerry wants to use the lav – says it's urgent.

ALMÁSY

Where are we going, please?

SOLDIER

Up North, to the coast. Benghazi. Soon be
there. Get you a boat back home.

ALMÁSY *can't bear this news. The* SERGEANT *returns,
considers the request.*

SERGEANT

Go on then – you take him. I've been up and
down this bloody train all day.

Int. Train corridor, the desert. Day

The SOLDIER *pushes* ALMÁSY *along the corridor. They
arrive outside the lavatory. The* SOLDIER *is distracted for
a split second. Enough for* ALMÁSY *to elbow him savagely
in the stomach, winding him, before battering him with his
fists. He wraps his cuffs around the* SOLDIER'*s neck and –*

yanking them together and twisting — proceeds to strangle the young SOLDIER.

Int. Train, the desert. Evening

ALMÁSY *clambers over the guardrail and leaps off, tumbling into the desert sunset.*

Ext. Railway track, the desert. Evening

ALMÁSY, *silhouetted against the evening sky, hobbles back down the track, three hundred miles away from the dying* KATHARINE CLIFTON, *no way now of saving her. He is a tiny speck in the vast desert. His heart is broken. He sinks to his knees in despair.*

Int. The Patient's room. Night

THE PATIENT *is exhausted. He has said aloud what has tortured him. His failure to save* KATHARINE. *He looks at* CARAVAGGIO.

THE PATIENT
So yes. She died because of me. Because I loved her. Because I had the wrong name.

CARAVAGGIO
And you never got back to the cave?

Ext. Kufra oasis. Day

ALMÁSY *is uncovering the tarpaulin which has been protecting* MADOX's *Tiger Moth. Around are German soldiers, two of whom are bringing cans of gasoline toward the plane.*

THE PATIENT (o/s)
I did get back. I kept my promise. I was assisted

by the Germans. I had our expedition maps.
And after the British made me their enemy, I
gave their enemy our maps.

ALMÁSY *carries a mapcase and hands it over to the*
German officer, who salutes him and walks toward his
car. ALMÁSY *turns to the plane, rips off a sign* MADOX
has pinned to a wing. It reads SEE YOU IN DORSET.

THE PATIENT (o/s)
So I got back to the desert and to Katharine in
Madox's English plane with German gasoline.
When I arrived in Italy, on my medical chart,
they wrote 'English Patient'. Isn't that funny,
after all that I became English.

Int. The Patient's room. Day

CARAVAGGIO *is looking out the window, his mind racing,*
his resolve evaporating.

CARAVAGGIO
You get to the morning and the poison leaks
away, doesn't it? Black nights. I thought I would
kill you.

THE PATIENT
You can't kill me. I died years ago.

CARAVAGGIO
No, I can't kill you now.

Above them, in her room, HANA *stands, having heard it*
all, the whole story; the whole puzzle finally in place.

Ext. The monastery. Approaching dawn

KIP has pulled out all of HARDY's gear. Now he starts on the tent, kicking at the pegs, collapsing it. HANA comes out into the garden, to join him. She says nothing.

KIP
We've been posted. North of Florence.

Now he's trying to fold a shirt. HANA takes it from him. She folds it.

KIP
I was thinking yesterday – yesterday! – the Patient and Hardy: they're everything that's good about England. I couldn't even say what that was. We didn't exchange two personal words, and we've been together through some terrible things, some terrible things.
> (*still incredulous*)
He was engaged to a girl in the village! – I mean –
> (*looks at HANA*)
– and us – he never once . . . He didn't ask me if I could spin the ball at cricket or the Kama Sutra or – I don't even know what I'm talking about.

HANA
You loved him.

Ext. (Near the) Base Camp at the Cave of Swimmers, 1942. Day

The familiar cleft in the rocks. The Tiger Moth lands.

Int. Cave of Swimmers. Torchlight

A flashlight flickers in the cave. ALMÁSY *appears.*

KATHARINE'*s corpse lies where he left her – a ghost on a bed of silk and blankets. The chill of the cave has preserved her. She could be asleep.*

ALMÁSY

Katharine.

He sobs, whispering to her. He's terribly cold, exhausted. He slips underneath the covers to be next to her, and closes his eyes.

Int. The Patient's room. Morning

HANA *sits with* THE ENGLISH PATIENT – *the room shuttered against the morning light. His breathing is*

noticeably worsening, a shudder of a breath, the shallow rise and fall of his chest hardly perceptible. HANA frets, touches his wrist, feeling for the pulse.

THE PATIENT

I'm still here.

HANA

You'd better be.

THE PATIENT

Don't depend on it. Will you? That little bit of air, in my lungs, each day gets less and less, which is all right, which is quite all right. I've been speaking to Caravaggio, my research assistant. He tells me there's a ghost in the cloisters. I can join him.

HANA is distracted by the sound of KIP's motorbike.

KIP (o/s)
(distant)

Hana.

THE PATIENT

It's the boy.

Ext. The monastery. Day

KIP sits on the motorbike, waiting for HANA. She goes to him, stands, fastens the top button of his coat. You feel she might just climb on the seat behind him. But she doesn't. Neither of them can think what to say.

HANA

I'll always go back to that church. Look at my painting.

KIP

I'll always go back to that church.

HANA

So one day we'll meet.

He nods, winds up the throttle, and is gone. HANA walks back to THE PATIENT's room.

Int. The Patient's room. Day

HANA *picks up the hypodermic to prepare his injection. She takes a vial.* THE PATIENT *is watching her. He reaches out and pushes two more vials toward her. Their eyes meet, then he shovels another, then all of them. She looks at him. It's a massive lethal dose.*

HANA *decides, starts to prepare the injection, her eyes filling with tears.* THE PATIENT *nods, smiles, whispers.*

THE PATIENT

Thank you.

She holds the loaded syringe up to the light. She's sobbing violently. THE PATIENT's *expression is full of peace.*

THE PATIENT

Read to me, will you? Read me to sleep.

Int. The Patient's room. Day

HANA *lies beside* THE ENGLISH PATIENT. *She has the Herodotus and is reading to him from the passage* KATHARINE *had written in his book as she waited for him in the Cave of Swimmers.*

(reading)

'My darling, I'm waiting for you. How long is a
day in the dark? or a week? The fire is gone now
and I'm horribly cold.'

The reading continues, but sometimes it's KATHARINE'S
own voice that's heard.

HANA

'I really ought to drag myself outside – but then
there would be the sun. I'm afraid I waste the
light on the paintings and on writing these
words. We die, we die rich with lovers and
tribes, tastes we have swallowed . . . bodies we
have entered and swum up like rivers, fears we
have hidden in like this wretched cave . . .'

Int. The Cave of Swimmers. Torchlight

ALMÁSY *smudges* KATHARINE's *pale face with saffron from the thimble. He presses his cheek to hers, smoothes her hair, with incredible tenderness.*

KATHARINE (o/s)
. . . I want all this marked on my body. We are the real countries, not the boundaries drawn on maps with the names of powerful men . . .

Ext. Cave of Swimmers. Day

ALMÁSY *comes out of the cave, carrying the bundle of* KATHARINE *in his arms, wrapped in the silks of her parachute. He's shuddering in the throes of his grief, but there's no sound.*

KATHARINE (o/s)
. . . I know you will come and carry me out into the palace of winds . . . That's all I've wanted – to walk in such a place with you, with friends, an earth without maps.

Int. The Patient's room. Day

THE PATIENT *is slipping away as* HANA *reads the last of* KATHARINE's *message.*

HANA
'The lamp's gone out . . . and I'm writing in the darkness.'

She looks up from the book. His eyes roll, his breathing quiets, then stops.

Ext. Lane outside the monastery garden. Day

CARAVAGGIO *is at the gate to the monastery. A truck is*

waiting with him. A family sits in the back of the truck.
CARAVAGGIO *stands with a young woman. He shouts
into the garden.*

> CARAVAGGIO
>
> Hana!

Int. The Patient's room. Day

HANA *lingers in the empty room. The mattress stripped
bare. No sign of their stay.*

> CARAVAGGIO (o/s)
>
> Hana, come on! Hana!

HANA *makes to leave, then sees the* Herodotus, *lying on
the bedside cabinet, and scoops it up.*

Ext. Lane outside monastery garden. Day

HANA *comes out to the truck, carrying the small bundle of
her belongings.* CARAVAGGIO *makes some introductions,
beginning with the woman driver,* GIOIA. *She and*
CARAVAGGIO *smile like lovers.*

> CARAVAGGIO
>
> Hana – this is Gioia.

GIOIA *smiles, shakes* HANA's *hand.*

> HANA
>
> Buon giorno.

> CARAVAGGIO
>
> She'll take you as far as Florence.

> HANA
>
> I can get in the back.

And she clambers up, sits down between the children. They exchange some small, stiff, shy smiles, and then the truck bounces away. HANA takes one final look at the monastery as it disappears around the bend and then turns and confronts the life insisting noisily in the truck.

Int. Tiger Moth. Day

Inside the cockpit: the couple as at the front of the film. ALMÁSY, obliterated by goggles and helmet, KATHARINE ahead of him, slumped forward as if sleeping.

The plane banks over the dark ravines of the Gilf Kebir, and then suddenly, the rocks have gone, giving way to the earth without maps – the desert – stretching out for mile after mile. ALMÁSY, THE ENGLISH PATIENT, looks down on it.

THE END

MIRAMAX FILMS

Presents
A SAUL ZAENTZ Production
An ANTHONY MINGHELLA Film

RALPH FIENNES
JULIETTE BINOCHE
WILLEM DAFOE
KRISTIN SCOTT THOMAS

The English Patient

Naveen Andrews
Colin Firth
Julian Wadham
Jürgen Prochnow
Kevin Whately
Clive Merrison
Nino Castelnuovo
Hichem Rostom
Peter Rühring

Film Editor Walter Murch, A.C.E.
Casting Michelle Guish and David Rubin, C.S.A.
Costume Designer Ann Roth
Line Producer Alessandro von Normann
Executive Producers Bob Weinstein, Harvey Weinstein and Scott Greenstein
Associate Producers Paul Zaentz and Steve Andrews
Original Music Gabriel Yared
Production Designer Stuart Craig
Director of Photography John Seale, A.C.S.
Based on the Novel by Michael Ondaatje
Screenplay by Anthony Minghella
Produced by Saul Zaentz
Directed by Anthony Minghella

END CREDITS

The Cast

Almásy	Ralph Fiennes
Hana	Juliette Binoche
Caravaggio	Willem Dafoe
Katharine Clifton	Kristin Scott Thomas
Kip	Naveen Andrews
Geoffrey Clifton	Colin Firth
Madox	Julian Wadham
Major Muller	Jürgen Prochnow
Hardy	Kevin Whately
Fenelon-Barnes	Clive Merrison
D'Agostino	Nino Castelnuovo
Fouad	Hichem Rostom
Bermann	Peter Rühring
Oliver	Geordie Johnson
Mary	Torri Higginson
Jan	Liisa Repo-Martell
Rupert Douglas	Raymond Coulthard
Corporal Dade	Philip Whitchurch
Spalding	Lee Ross
Beach Interrogation Officer	Anthony Smee
Young Canadian Soldier	Matthew Ferguson
Kiss Me Soldier	Jason Done
Sergeant, Desert Train	Roger Morlidge
Private, Desert Train	Simon Sherlock
Interrogation Room Soldiers	Sebastian Schipper, Fritz Eggert
Arab Nurse	Sonia Mankai
Aicha	Rim Turki
Officer in Square	Sebastian Rudolph
Interpreter in Square	Thoraya Sehill
Woman with Baby in Square	Sondess Belhassen
Officer, El Taj	Dominic Mafham
Corporal, El Taj	Gregor Truter
Bedouin Doctor	Salah Miled
Ancient Arab	Abdellatif Hamrouni
Kamal	Samy Azaiez
Al Auf	Habib Chetoui
Officer's Wife	Phillipa Day
Lady Hampton	Amanda Walker
Sir Ronnie Hampton	Paul Kant

While a number of the characters who appear in this film are based on historical figures, and while many of the areas described – such as the Cave of Swimmers and its surrounding desert – exist, and were explored in the 1930s, it is important to stress that this story is a fiction and that the portraits of the characters who appear in it are fictional, as are some of the events and journeys.

Unit Production Managers Franco Ballati, Lynn Kamern
First Assistant Director Steve Andrews
Second Assistant Director Emma Schofield
Make-up Fabrizio Sforza
Prosthetics by Jim Henson's Creature Shop
Co-Costume Designer Gary Jones
Canadian Casting Deirdre Bowen
German Casting Risa Kes
Assistant Directors Luigi Vallini, Andrea Girolami
Script Supervisor Dianne Dreyer
Production Coordinator Daniela Vecchi
Production Coordinator, Rome & Viareggio Judith Goodman
Production Coordinator, Rome Francesca Cingolani
Assistant Production Coordinators Holly Hardin, Silvia Ranfagni
Production Secretary Maria Grazia Melline
Production Assistants Francesca Spinotti, Aminta Townshend
Assistant to Mr Zaentz Nancy Eichler
Assistant to Mr Minghella Sarah Ewing
Assistant to Mr Fiennes Becky Veduccio
Assistant to Ms Binoche Lena Martins
Dialogue Coach, Ms Binoche Vernice Klier
Unit Publicist Larry Kaplan
Still Photographer Phil Bray
Choreographer Carolyn Choa
1st Camera Operator John Seale
1st Camera Assistant Robert De Nigris
2nd Camera Operator/Steadicam Daniele Massaccesi
2nd Camera Assistant Robert De Angelis
Camera Loader Antonello Emidi
Video Playback Maurizio Lorenzetti, Derin Seale
Sound Recordists Chris Newman, Ivan Sharrock, C.A.S.
Boom Operators Marc Jon Sullivan, Donald Banks
Sound Assistant Adriano Di Lorenzo

Gaffer Mo Flam
Best Boy Stefano Marino
Key Grip Tommaso Mele
Rigging Grip Michele Mele
Grips Sergio Faina, Carlo Postiglione, Massimiliano Dessena, Gianpaolo Majorana, Franco Mele
Rigging Gaffer Guiseppe Meloni
Electricians Marcello Perricone, Maurizio Di Stefano, Alberto Rogante, Daniele Cafolla, Severino Tramontani, Michele Pellegrini, Salvatore Ruberto
Generator Operator Mario Lamoratta
Art Director & Set Decorator Aurelio Crugnola
Assistant Art Directors Neil Lamont, Franco Fumagalli
Set Decorator Stephenie McMillan
Assistant Set Decorators Alessandra Querzola, John Bush
Art Department Standby/Research Lucinda Thompson
Art Department Assistants Stefano Pessione, Stefania D'Amario
Production Assistant Michele Papa
Fresco Painter Paola Mugnai
Assistant Fresco Painters Bruno Ranieri, Remo Sperati
Scenic Artists Brian Bishop, Doug Bishop
Draftsman Giulia Chiara Crugnola
Translite Backings Alan White
Storyboard Artist Tony Wright
Painters Luciano Curti, Paul Wescot
Standby Painters Mick Rossman, Steve Clark
Desert Cars Art Director Stuart Rose
Construction Coordinator Luigi Quintilli
Construction Manager Romano Bellucci
Construction Supervisor, Tunisia Francesco Pizzonia
Property Master Tony Teiger
Assistant Property Master, Tunisia Ty Teiger
Standby Props Bernie Hearn, Roberto Magagnini
Dressing Props Francesco Postiglione, Maurizio Iacopelli, Mauro Nati, Luciano Magagnini, Peter Watson
Assistant to the Costume Designer Carlo Poggioli
Key Costumers Iris Horta Lemos, Donna Maloney, Tim McKelvy
Costumers Salvatore Salzano, Adriana Mattiozzi
Seamstresses Gabriella Generosi, Franca Rotondo
Research Hannah Green

Ms Binoche & Ms Scott Thomas Make-up Louise Constad
Make-up Artists Alessandra Sampaolo, Guiseppe Desiato, Antonio Maltempo
Chief Hairstylist Giusi Bovino
Hairdresser Elisabetta de Leonardis

For Jim Henson's Creature Shop
Visual Supervisor John Stephenson
Creative Project Supervisor Neal Scanlan
Production Supervisor Karen Cassie
English Patient Prosthetic Make-up Nigel Booth
Sculptors Jeremy Hunt, Graham High
Artwork Marion Appleton
Animatronics Design Vincent Abbott, Jason Read, Andy Roberts
Fabrication Sam Broadbent, Tamzine Hanks, Louisa Jordan, Esteban Mendoza
Hair Design Val Jones
Mold Design Supervisor Kenny Wilson
Moldmakers Barry Folwer, Terry Sibley, Mel Coleman, Terry James
Chargehand Dave Kelly
Foam Department Marie Fraser, Karina Randall, Adrian Getley, Andy Lees
Silicone Department Kelly Sant
Optician Chris Edmond

Location Managers Giorgio Gallani, Fabiomassimo Dell'Orco, Annette Carducci
Assistant Location Managers Christina de'Rossi, Lorenzo Errico
Production Auditor Enzo Sisti
Production Accountant Maria Fiorito
Accountant Karin Mercurio
Payroll Accountant Giorgio Catalano
Production Accountant, Tunisia Giorio Tregnaghi
Accounting Assistant Salvatore Magnisi
U.S. Production Office Fredrica Drotos, Rob Lloyd
Special Vehicle Coordinator Duncan Barbour
Armorers: Tuscany Aldo Gasparri
Sahara Desert Carl Schmidt
Special Effects Supervisor Richard Conway

Senior Effects Technicians Tim Willis, David Eltham
Senior Effects Technician, Italy Giancarlo Mancini
Effects Crew Sam Conway, Fausto Baldinelli, Francesco Sabelli, Raffaele Battistelli, Paul Stentiford
Visual Effects by Digital Film, London
Visual Effects Supervisor Dennis Lowe
Facilities Producer Matthew Holben
Digital Line Producer Arthur Windus
Assistant Producer Matthew Plummer
VFX Designers Richard Bain, Charlie Noble, Paul Riddle, Mark Stannard, Frazer Churchill
C.G. Designers Keith Roberts, Julian Mann, Andy Hall
Film Outputting Ian Chisholm

Aerial Unit

Airplane Coordinator Pino Valenti
Pilot, Madox's Tiger Moth Clive Watson
Pilot, Clifton's Stearman Franco Actis
Helicopter Pilots Giancarlo Giunchi, Marco Besagni
Mechanics Sergio Arban, Terry Bridle

Stunt Supervisor Jim Dowdall
Stunt Coordinator Franco Salomon
Stuntmen Paul Heasman, Lee Sheward, Julian Spencer, Steve Street-Griffin, Riccardo Mioni
Transportation Manager Andrea Borella
Catering: Italy Organizzazione Cucine Mobili
Tunisia Le Gourmet
Nursing Consultant Brenda Fuller
Demolitions Consultant Major Arthur Hogben

Tunisian Crew

International Monastir Films Fiscal Representative Ridha Turki
Unit Manager Hamid Elleuch
Assistant Directors Mouez Kamoun, Meriem Beschaouch, Moslah Kraiem
Location Managers Brahim Toumi, Leila Turki, Abdelijabar Ayadi, Mouldi Essaidi, Mokhtar Joulak
Accountant Ridha Taya
Production Coordinator Amel Becharnia
Production Secretary Mounira Chebbah

Production Assistant Aziz Ben Chaabane
Grips Lassad Ben Khelifa, Imed Nouira
Electricians Adelaziz Belgaied, Nejib Sriha, Mohamed Gharbi
Assistant Art Director Taieb Jallouli
Assistant Set Dresser Mohsen Rais
Prop Master Mohamed Bergaoui
Prop Buyer Kamel Riabi
Assistant Props Jamel Bizid, Mohamed Trimeche
Wardrobe Assistants Lilia Lakhoua, Amel Helali, Kamel
Marmouche, Montacer Skhiri
Transportation Manager Mahmoud Ben Dhifallah
Make-up & Hair Assistants Ferid Sfaxi, Mustapha Ben
Chaabane
Set Doctor Adel Marzouki
Set Nurse Riadh Chouanine

Second Unit
Director Peter Markham
Director of Photography Remi Adefarasin, B.S.C.
First Assistant Director Gianni Arduini
Second Assistant Director Andrea Marrari
Script Supervisor Rachel Griffiths
Focus Puller Vincenzo Carpineta
Camera Loader/Video Playback Cristina Capone
Production Coordinator Gabriella Di Santo
Production Assistant, Trieste Dino Castelli
Accountant Alberto De Stefani
Sound Mixer Gianni Sardo
Props Bruce Cheeseman
Set Costumer Alfredo Bocci
Hair & Make-up Maria Rizzo
Grip Giampaolo Bagala

Post Production Crew
Associate Editor Pat Jackson
Post Production Supervisor and 1st Asst AVID Editor Edie
Bleiman
1st Assistant Film Editors Rosmary Conte, Daniel Farrell
Assistant Film Editors Robert Grahamjones, Robin Lee, Scott
Guitteau, Jeffery Stephens, Franca Silvi
Apprentice Editor Sean Cullen
Supervising Sound Editor Pat Jackson

1st Assistant Sound Editor Marilyn S. Zalkan

Sound Effects Editors Kyrsten Mate Comoglio, Douglas S. Murray, Jennifer L. Ware

Assistant Sound Effects Editors Stephen Kearney, Aura Belle Gilge

Dialogue Editors Sara Bolder, John Nutt, Dianna Stirpe

Assistant Dialogue Editors David Franklin Bergad, Tobin Delaca Davis, Mary Works

ADR Supervisor Mark Levinson

ADR Editor Richard Quinn

Apprentice Sound Editor Michael Axinn

Foley Editor Malcolm Fife

Foley Mixer Richard Duarte

Assistant Foley Mixer Steve Fontano

Foley Artists Margie O'Malley, Marnie Moore, Jennifer Myers

Rerecording Mixers Walter Murch, Mark Berger, David Parker

Music Premixer Michael Semanick

Loop Group Voice Casting Brendan Donnison

Sound Transfers Rome Liberata Zocchi

Telecine Operators Harris Leibowitz, Glenn Kasprzycki

Original Music Recorded by the *Academy of St Martin in the Fields*

Harry Rabinowitz, Conductor

John Constable, Piano Soloist

Recorded at Air Studios, London and YAD Music, France.
Music Sound Designer, Georges Rodi;
Recording Engineer, Keith Grant

Shepheard's Hotel Jazz Orchestra recorded at Angel Recording Studios, London.
Conducted and Arranged by Ronnie Hazelhurst
Sound Engineer, John Timperley

Music Editor Robert Randles
Assistant Music Editor Ling Ling Li

The Saul Zaentz Film Center Staff

Jim Austin	Loren Byer	Frank Canonica
Vince Casper	Amanda Chan	Grant Foerster
Anne Geyer	Rich Kahn	Michael Kelly
Scott Levitin	Kathy McVey	Dan Olmsted

Jim Pasque   Mark Paul   Scott Roberts
David Roesch   Roy Segal   Steve Shurtz
Greg Simon   Joe Tysl   Laurie Wentworth
Jeff Whittle

The Producer and Director Wish to Thank:

Convento di Sant'Anna   The Royal Geographic
                                    Society
Comune di Pienza   The British Library
Croce Rossa Italiana   British Pathe
Hotel des Bains, Lido di Venezia   G. H. Mumm & Cie
Comune di Trieste   Anderson & Sheppard
The Tunisian Government   Angels & Bermans
   & the Tozeur District Governor   Costumi Tirelli
Tunis Air   Steppin' Out

Cameras and Lenses Provided by Panavision SRL
Cranes and Dollies Provided by Cinecittà Film Studios and
   F.lli Cartocci, Rome
Negative Developed at Cinecittà Film Studios, Rome
Sound Transferred at Cinecittà Film Studios, Rome
Negative Cutter: Gary Burritt
Color Timer Bill Pine
Color by deluxe
Prints by deluxe toronto
Title Design by Deborah Ross Film Design
Main Title by Digital Film Animation, London
End Titles by Pacific Title

SOUNDTRACK RECORDING AVAILABLE ON FANTASY
INC.

DOLBY DIGITAL IN SELECTED THEATRES

All film editing, sound editing, and Dolby Digital mix com-
pleted at THE SAUL ZAENTZ FILM CENTER, Berkeley,
California

Yes! We Have No Bananas
Words and Music by Frank Silver and Irving Conn.
Published by Skidmore Music Co., Inc.

Where Or When
Words and Music by Richard Rodgers and Lorenz Hart.
Published by Williamson Music, Inc. & Chappell & Co.

Flat Foot Floogee
Words & Music by Slim Gaillard, Slam Stewart & Bud Green.
Published by Jewel Music Publishing Co.,
ASCAP and Holliday Publications ASCAP.

It's Only A Paper Moon
Words and Music by Billy Rose, E.Y. Harburg and Harold Arlen.
Published by Warner Bros., Inc. & Chappell & Co.,
S.A. Music Co., and Glocca Morra Music Corp.

Szerelem, Szerelem
Performed by Muzsikás featuring Márta Sebestyén.
Arranged by Karoly Cserepes. Published by Rykomusic (ASCAP).
Courtesy of Hannibal Records, a Rykodisc label.

Cheek to Cheek
Words & Music by Irving Berlin. Irving Berlin Music Company.
Performed by Fred Astaire. Courtesy of Columbia Records by arrangement with Sony Music Licensing and Mrs Fred Astaire.
Performed by Ella Fitzgerald. Courtesy of Verve Records by arrangement with Polygram Film & TV Licensing.

Wang Wang Blues
Words by Leo Wood. Music by Gus Mueller, 'Buster' Johnson and Henry Busse.
Published by Cromwell Music, Inc., EMI Feist Catalog Inc., and Bienstock Publishing Co., on behalf of Redwood Music Ltd.
Performed by Benny Goodman. Courtesy of Columbia Records by arrangement with Sony Music Licensing.

Pettin' In The Park
Words by Al Dubin. Music by Harry Warren.
Published by Warner Bros., Inc. Courtesy of Turner Entertainment Co. From 'Gold Diggers of 1933'.

Manhattan
Words by Lorenz Hart. Music by Richard Rodgers.
Published by Edward B. Marks Music Company.

One O'Clock Jump
Music by William 'Count' Basie.

Printed in the United Kingdom
by Lightning Source UK Ltd.
101200UKS00001BA/20